LIST OF CHARACTERS

Participants:
ARIA ALAGHA
ARCHIE ALEXANDER-SINCLAIR
MEECHY
HAYLEY NEWMAN
PIPPA NORTH
EDNA READ
MICHAEL STANLEY & KIDS
LUCY TURNER
AARON WILLIAMSON
JEREMY WOOD (GPS DRAWING GUY)

Drivers:
MARK CUTLER & SON KYLE
FRED DEDMAN
IAN MARSHALL
TONY WHITE

Effigy:
TIM

Camera:
JUSTIN NEAL

Abbreviations

ext   exterior
int   interior
pov   point of view
os   off-screen

1 EXT MILTON KEYNES GALLERY—NIGHT.

A group of people gather in front of a white coach.

PARTICIPANTS: *ad lib indistinct chatter.*

2 INT COACH.

TIM *gets on the coach—he carries an effigy of himself.*

TIM: Hi, this is my dummy.

TONY: Everyone should have one.

TIM *is seen from behind as he puts his effigy in its seat before leaving the coach.*

TONY *the driver is sitting in the driving seat waiting to leave— the* PARTICIPANTS *get on the coach—they are all carrying bags and there is a general kerfuffle as they settle down.*

TONY: Are you all doing this voluntarily?

PIPPA: Yes.

EDNA: They all think I'm mad, and I probably am.

    TONY *turns to* HAYLEY.

TONY: Are you ready?

HAYLEY: Take it away, Tony.

    The lights on the dashboard flicker—TONY *starts the coach and switches the radio on*—*'Wild Thing' plays.*

Lucy's Diary
9:30 pm: I'm not sure what my expectations were but it's not what I imagined. It's a posh bus with tables and plenty of space.

The story and characters depicted in this screenplay were part of the Milton Keynes Gallery offsite event MKVH (Milton Keynes Vertical Horizontal) *which took place between 28 March and 1 April 2006.*

0 mins

3 EXT MILTON KEYNES GALLERY.

Coach pulls away.

Fade in superimposed title: MILTON KEYNES GALLERY presents

Fade out title.

Fade in superimposed title: MKVH

Fade out title.

Fade in superimposed title: by HAYLEY NEWMAN

Fade out title.

The camera trucks alongside coach.

Fade in superimposed title: Starring (in alphabetical order)

Fade out title.

Fade in superimposed title:
ARIA ALAGHA
ARCHIE ALEXANDER-SINCLAIR
KYLE CUTLER
MEECHY
HAYLEY NEWMAN
PIPPA NORTH
EDNA READ
MICHAEL STANLEY & KIDS
LUCY TURNER

AARON WILLIAMSON
JEREMY WOOD (GPS DRAWING GUY)

Fade out title.

Fade in superimposed title: Drivers (in order of appearance)
TONY WHITE
MARK CUTLER
IAN MARSHALL
FRED DEDMAN

Fade out title.

Fade in superimposed title: Video documentation by
JUSTIN NEAL

Fade out title.

Fade in superimposed title: Production Manager
EMMA DEAN

Fade out title.

Fade in superimposed title: Produced by
MILTON KEYNES GALLERY

Fade out title.

Fade in superimposed title: Written and conceived by
HAYLEY NEWMAN

Title fades out.

Music fades out.

15 mins

30/03/2006   21:53:51   61 kph

4 INT COACH.

The PARTICIPANTS *gather round two tables—*AARON *sits to the side of the group—the light inside the coach is dim.*

MEECHY: Are you our artist?

HAYLEY: Yeah …

MEECHY: Are we literally going to just drive around the grid?

HAYLEY: Yeah …

MEECHY: It's a road trip.

HAYLEY *receives a text message.*

HAYLEY: Someone just sent a message congratulating us on leaving!

The camera pans round the individual faces of the PARTICIPANTS *as they introduce themselves—it finally rests on* HAYLEY.

HAYLEY: So I'm Hayley Newman. This is Aaron, my partner. He's going to be providing musical inspiration on the trip. He's deaf. This is Jeremy who's doing a GPS drawing of our journey. Meechy, you are from Milton Keynes, aren't you? Edna, Lucy, Pippa, Archie and Aria – I think most of you are from Milton Keynes. Sorry, Lucy is from Barnham. But most people are from here. Uhh, that is Tim at the back.

HAYLEY *turns and points to the effigy at the back of the bus.*

30 mins

MEECHY: Are all the troublemakers at the back?

HAYLEY: Tim couldn't come, so he made this effigy of himself. His spirit will haunt the coach more than he ever could.

ALL: Hello, Tim.

Everyone is quiet as HAYLEY *begins to explain the* MKVH *project.*

HAYLEY: I'm just going to explain the ideas behind *MKVH*.

MEECHY: It has to be brief.

HAYLEY: Right, we've only got thirty hours … Mike asked me to come to Milton Keynes and talk to him about doing a project here. We spoke about an idea that I had had for some time, which was to drive a bus until it ran out of fuel. The fact that Milton Keynes has been built around an American-style grid system made it more appealing to do the project here. It gives the trip a sense of boredom, containment and involves going nowhere. *MKVH* is a vehicle (excuse the pun) for generating conversation both on and off the bus.

I am interested in us experiencing the length of the trip, the main focus of which is the moment the coach runs out of diesel. I suppose we just have to wait for that to happen, which is inevitable, unless the world ends or the coach breaks down first.

We are going to be on the coach for around thirty hours. There will be breaks, so if people want to stop anywhere in particular we can.

45 mins

MEECHY: You should have put a bet on it.

HAYLEY: I did try. Mike and I went to Ladbrokes, but we were too late.

AARON: A durational performance is very much about what you are feeling while you are doing it. So, the work isn't Hayley's performance it is our experience of doing it.

EDNA *and* HAYLEY *sit left and right.*

EDNA: I thought this would have been like *Big Brother* and we would be trapped on the coach.

HAYLEY: No, it is freer than that.

EDNA: I needn't have brought all my stuff.

EDNA *looks down and points at two large brown leather bags.*

EDNA: I went to America with those and now I am going to spend two nights on this bus!

HAYLEY: I thought that you were a bit over-prepared when you arrived.

1 hr

> AARON *puts two bottles of wine and four bottles of beer on the table.*

PIPPA: I thought we weren't allowed any alcohol on the trip?

> JEREMY *opens a bottle of wine and offers people a drink.*

> HAYLEY *and* ARIA *sit talking—*ARIA *has the beginnings of a beard that he will continue to grow over the next couple of days—he fidgets in his seat.*

ARIA: It's like a 'Magical Mystery Tour'.

HAYLEY: It is, yes.

ARIA: Did anyone watch that? I used to travel lots. Most of the people I know are from abroad.

HAYLEY: It is weird to think about international travel when we are stuck driving round Milton Keynes on an intercontinental coach.

ARIA: (*Looks out of the window and breathes hard.*) I wanna get distracted from the real world.

> JEREMY, MEECHY *and* EDNA *are seated together.*

JEREMY: The layout of Milton Keynes was designed on a computer.

MEECHY: Yeah, that's true.

> MEECHY *pauses.*

MEECHY: Has it changed now?

EDNA: I'm not saying it's a bad thing, but things have changed from the early days.

Int/ext—window—distorted trees are seen in silhouette against the night sky.

1 hr 15 mins

30/03/2006   22:53:01   23 kph

MEECHY draws and speaks at the same time.

MEECHY: How do you get to a position where you say I want to drive a bus around Milton Keynes until it runs out of petrol?

ARIA: That is a good question actually. Who do you know, high up?

HAYLEY: I spoke to many people about doing this and lots said no, until Mike said yes. He gave me my break.

The table-top is covered with paper, pens, books, plastic cups and bottles.

MEECHY: I'm surprised you were allowed to do this.

HAYLEY: I rang around a few people …

ARIA: The question?

HAYLEY: 'Could I hire a coach that gets driven until it runs out of petrol?'

ARIA: Response?

HAYLEY: 'No way, love.'

General laughter.

HAYLEY: New City Coaches said yes.

The coach stops at a run-down coach station—there are a few people waiting—it is late and unclear if any coaches are still running.

EDNA: The worst place in Milton Keynes?

TONY: Wonderful place, this. I haven't stopped here for years.

5 EXT MILTON KEYNES COACHWAY.

Some of the participants get off the coach for a break—they huddle together in front of the coach.

Lucy's Diary
11 pm: I haven't had a 'what the hell am I doing here?' moment yet. There's a dummy called Tim because the real Tim couldn't come.

1 hr 30 mins

30/03/2006   23:08:59   0.23 kph

   6 INT COACH.

   TONY *turns and talks to* HAYLEY.

TONY: How many of you are there?

HAYLEY: (*Counting.*) One, two, three, four, five, six, seven, eight, … nine.

   TONY *switches the engine on and begins to drive.*

MEECHY: What is your impression of Milton Keynes?

HAYLEY: In a way it is attractive. There is space here.

MEECHY: If you want to get around the place it is easy.

   ARIA *drinks red wine and* LUCY *doodles on a scrap of paper.*

ARIA: I saw something in the paper – it said 'Volunteer for bus journey'. I said, 'Shit, that's for me. Just call it. I *have* to go.'

   ARIA *puts down his plastic cup as the coach turns a corner— the cup wobbles but does not spill.*

LUCY: Unfortunately and maybe stereotypically, there are lots of roundabouts!

   Both laugh.

LUCY: I came because I just wanted the experience.

1 hr 45 mins

30/03/2006   23:23:02   26 kph

HAYLEY'S phone rings—it is JUSTIN—he is in his car trying to find the coach so he can video it as it is driven round Milton Keynes—he asks where the coach is—HAYLEY peers out of the window and looks for a street sign to indicate where they are.

HAYLEY: We are just approaching the Leadenhall Roundabout. I think we are going along H7–V7?

ARIA points at another coach that he sees from the window.

ARIA: Look, Koncept Travel!

HAYLEY: No, *we* are conceptual travel!

General laughter.

HAYLEY: Koncept Travel wanted too much money.

ARIA: Theoretically it would have been great.

The sound of a car horn is heard os—JEREMY is surprised.

JEREMY: Was he tooting us?

2 hrs

30/03/2006   23:38:03   67 kph

Int/ext road—the tarmac road is wet and shiny.

JEREMY: Are you trying to do a spiral now?

TONY: I was doing a spiral, but we have just come off of it.

HAYLEY *looks at the hand-held GPS unit.*

HAYLEY: Oh look at that, we have got it on this drawing.
(*To* JEREMY.) I really liked your GPS drawing site. I didn't know
about the Frieze Art Fair project before.

JEREMY: It was just me being the map man. Apparently I am
known as the 'GPS Guy'.

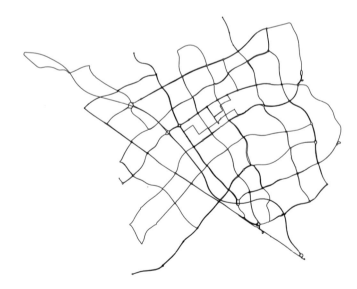

2 hrs 15 mins

The camera slowly pans right before resting on ARIA'S *face—he looks up and pretends to be in agony.*

ARIA: I know I'm going to regret this.

PIPPA, EDNA *and* MEECHY *sit talking—they are viewed from behind.*

PIPPA: I still don't know Milton Keynes.

EDNA: You'll have enough time tomorrow. We are going to go round and round.

MEECHY: Are there some nibbles here?

HAYLEY *takes out three elaborately wrapped boxes.*

Lucy's Diary
12 midnight: Going to the toilet while the bus goes round roundabouts is hilarious.

2 hrs 30 mins

MEECHY *holds out a bottle of wine—*AARON *and* ARIA *sit next to each other—they are laughing.*

MEECHY: (*To* AARON.) Would you like some more wine?

AARON: There isn't much there.

Os—the sound of a bottle rolling around the floor of the coach.

MEECHY: It wasn't mine!

Os—the sound of bottles clinking.

MEECHY: I thought it said somewhere that you couldn't drink on the coach? You know what the headline in the newspaper will be, Aria? 'Drunken Debauchery!'

ARIA: I'd only buy it if it were about myself.

Int/ext—road—there are no streetlights and it is dark and difficult to see anything other than the white lines on the road.

TONY: Total eclipse of the streetlights round here.

HAYLEY: There appears to be a power cut and all the streetlights have gone.

MEECHY *makes a mock accusation at* HAYLEY.

MEECHY: Is this part of your thing? Did you arrange it?

2 hrs 45 mins

> EDNA *and* HAYLEY *sit on the back seat of the coach—they speak in hushed tones—*EDNA *appears to be tired.*

EDNA: Hope you don't mind me taking over the back seat.

HAYLEY: No, not at all.

EDNA: I'm going to get my stuff organised.

> EDNA *slowly opens her bag and carefully begins to unpack her things.*

> *The bag contains: a toilet bag, wipes, a bottle of water, chocolate, apples, muesli bars, a diary, writing paper, a note pad and a book,* The Hitler Emigrés, *by Daniel Snowman.*

> EDNA *lays out her sleeping bag and small pillow on the back seat—she puts on a ski suit, gets into her bed and closes her eyes.*

3 hrs

> AARON *is excited—he jumps up and down in his seat—all his movements are exaggerated.*

AARON: Oh there is a donkey, I want to take a photograph of the donkey for posterity. It's around here somewhere.

JEREMY: Is he a concrete donkey like a concrete cow, or just a donkey?

> AARON *peers out of the coach window—he is looking for the donkey.*

AARON: It's coming up, I think he is coming up. I'm counting the laps. I think we are coming up to the donkey. He's on a chain, on a chain.

ARIA: Is he a real donkey?

AARON: Well, I don't know if he is a donkey. He may be a Gypsy's horse or something.

PIPPA: I keep seeing the horse.

3 hrs 15 mins

AARON: Let's see how long it takes to do a lap.

JEREMY stands behind TONY the driver.

JEREMY: Tony, are you doing laps at the moment?

TONY: No, I'm doing … What am I doing at the moment? I don't really know where we are.

JEREMY: Have you seen a donkey around here?

TONY: There was a small horse. It was tied up and it looked just like a pantomime horse. I know where it is.

JEREMY: Near here?

TONY: I went past three times before I realised it was a proper horse.

Int/ext road—the coach headlights illuminate the surrounding trees, hedgerows and road signs—they are like searchlights looking for the donkey.

3 hrs 30 mins

MEECHY: Has anyone got any drawing requests?

MEECHY, AARON *and* JEREMY *look at one of* MEECHY'S *drawings.*

MEECHY: An undersized monster.

AARON: Are you 'sinestre'?

MEECHY: Am I sinister?

AARON *shows his left palm to* MEECHY.

AARON: 'Sinestre' is another word for left-handed.

MEECHY: I think I should now draw the monster that makes the previous monster feel woefully inadequate. A 'monster's monster'.

*There is a pile of books and DVDs on the table—*HAYLEY *holds up one of the books.*

HAYLEY: Someone named Darren gave us this book for the journey.

ARIA: Who is Darren?

AARON *nonchalantly picks up a copy of the book that Darren has left for everyone to read.*

AARON: He's donated his book for us to read?

AARON *holds a copy of the* Easy Rider *DVD in the air.*

AARON: Actually I've got a tape from Madonna and have you seen this DVD that Dennis Hopper gave us?

JEREMY: Wishing us his luck.

HAYLEY: He sent it. We got it yesterday.

JEREMY: A special message from Dennis Hopper.

ARIA: 'GO GUYS'.

AARON *grins.*

AARON: 'You blew it man!'

3 hrs 45 mins

31/03/2006   01:23:05   69 kph

The position of the coach is indicated by a flashing dot moving around a map on the computer screen.

HAYLEY: Wow!

HAYLEY looks at the GPS drawing on the handset—she is transfixed by the drawing.

HAYLEY: Tony is being really systematic.

JEREMY: It's a sort of weaving idea. He did east-west. (*To* TONY.) Could you try a north-south weave?

TONY drives—he looks ahead and talks out of the side of his mouth.

TONY: We can do, but it isn't quite as straightforward, because two or three of the roads that run north-south don't run all the way through the city.

4 hrs

31/03/2006   01:38:01   68 kph

MEECHY *and* ARIA *are in deep conversation.*

MEECHY: If you think of disaster situations, do we save works of art or do we save food?

ARIA: Carry food perhaps?

MEECHY: And so in an event like that, food is more important.

AARON: The bus driver is going to tell us when we pass the donkey.

JEREMY: I've got it on the GPS. We can now tell when we are coming up to it.

JEREMY *peers out of the window.*

JEREMY: I'm beginning to recognise things.

TONY: (*Shouts.*) Coming up to the concrete cows.

Int/ext window—there are indistinguishable shapes in a field— voices continue os.

PIPPA: They are not lit up.

ALL: They should be.

TONY: In about two minutes we will get to the pantomime horse.

4 hrs 15 mins

31/03/2006　01:53:04　34 kph

    TONY *drives the coach round and round the roundabout.*

TONY: It looks like a pantomime horse. We are going round, we are going round. I'm just trying to confuse him. Do you have any preference where you would like to stop this morning?

HAYLEY: Not really, err … No. Somewhere nice?

JEREMY: Somewhere with a view?

    AARON *holds his camera up to the window and takes a photo of the donkey with a flash.*

4 hrs 30 mins

    PIPPA *sits foreground right and* AARON *background left.*

PIPPA: Are you a late night person?

AARON: Yeah, I am, yeah. I never really go to sleep early.

PIPPA: What time do you normally go to bed?

AARON: Well, most nights between midnight and 1 am.

PIPPA: That is early.

AARON: Early? What time do you go to bed?

PIPPA: About three.

AARON: In the morning? You're joking! What do you do until 3 am?

JEREMY: (*Os.*) Get some peace and quiet.

AARON: We are all going to be night owls on this trip. I'm going to sleep towards the end of it. I don't want to miss a minute.

    AARON *gets up and returns holding two bottles of whisky in the air.*

ARIA: Oh my god, what do you have there?

4 hrs 45 mins

PIPPA: I imagined there would be hundreds of people on here. It is great to have space. Such a luxury.

JEREMY *stands behind* TONY.

JEREMY: What is your plan for this route?

TONY: We are going north-south, but instead of doing every road, I'm doing every other one.

On the dashboard—green, orange, red and yellow lights flash— the speedometer moves from right to left as the coach accelerates and decelerates—the fuel gauge and milometer can also be seen.

TONY *and* JEREMY *continue to talk os.*

TONY: The gauge has started moving.

JEREMY: Not quite a millimetre, and not quite a fraction.

TONY: We have only actually done about one hundred and twenty miles.

JEREMY: Too many bloody roundabouts in the way. Do you reckon it is more fuel efficient driving this way?

TONY: Less, because of the amount of breaking, slowing down and accelerating. We are averaging about thirty miles per hour.

5 hrs

MEECHY: Would we not be stopping at Tesco's or something?

TONY: There is a Sainsbury's there. I'm going to pull over on this side so you won't be bothered by drunken people.

AARON *looks into his wine.*

AARON: Do you realise we are going to be on this bus tomorrow night as well?

The coach stops.

7 EXT ROADSIDE.

AARON, MEECHY, PIPPA, JEREMY, HAYLEY *and* ARIA *get off the coach—*ARIA *and* MEECHY *are in deep conversation.*

ARIA: 'Ride on Time' was my favourite song …

MEECHY: When you say 'House' people think (*Sings*) tststststst 'Fascinating Rhythm …', 'Ghetto Heaven …'.

ARIA *leans forward to light a cigarette.*

5 hrs 15 mins

8 INT COACH.

The PARTICIPANTS *get back onto the coach and begin to settle down—a few go to the back of the coach to get some sleep—* PIPPA, AARON, HAYLEY *and* JEREMY *continue talking.*

PIPPA: Do we have to find our own way home from where the bus breaks down?

AARON: What, how to get home?

AARON *turns to* HAYLEY.

AARON: Do you think Tony could drop us off in Whitechapel?

HAYLEY *looks at* AARON—*she smiles and shrugs her shoulders.*

JEREMY: Or just keep going? Why not fill her up again?

AARON: You should run a book or something. A fiver each. I reckon we are going to run out exactly where it is now.

The coach door closes—we hear the sound of the engine starting os.

5 hrs 30 mins

31/03/2006   03 : 08 : 00   67 kph

AARON *turns to* JEREMY.

AARON: You look like Peter Fonda.

HAYLEY: Yeah, man.

AARON: He does, doesn't he? If you had a bit more facial hair by your ears.

HAYLEY: You've got the glasses.

JEREMY: I don't think so.

HAYLEY *feigns outrage.*

HAYLEY: He was gorgeous, what are you saying?

JEREMY: Oh, OK.

AARON: You have got the same eyes.

Close-up on AARON.

AARON: Well, *Easy Rider* is an interesting film because loads of people that were half hippies suddenly became full hippies.

AARON *puts on a pair of sunglasses—he mimics being a hippy.*

AARON: I need to go on a road trip and I need to freak out.

AARON *stops pretending to be a hippy.*

AARON: If you look at the film closely it is actually saying that being a hippy is a load of bollocks. Revolution, baby! What about The Merry Pranksters – did you ever hear about them? About Neal Cassady and Jack Kerouac?

JEREMY: Yeah.

AARON *pours whisky into plastic cups.*

JEREMY: That's tough. It's a tour bus now.

AARON: It's Rock and Roll. There are too many tour buses.

AARON *and* JEREMY *clink plastic and drink a shot of whisky.*

The radio is playing 'Stairway to Heaven'.

RADIO: 'And as we wind down the road, our shadows taller than our soul'.

5 hrs 45 mins

AARON *turns to his left and speaks to* HAYLEY.

AARON: 1982 – twenty-four years ago – I lived my life on buses.

RADIO: 'And if you listen very hard, the tune will come to you at last'.

HAYLEY: Where was that?

RADIO: 'When we are all one and one is all, to be a rock and not to roll'.

AARON: England mostly – Manchester, Sheffield. We used to drink a lot of JD. But that was many, many, many moons ago. This is very good, I really like disorientation. It would be nice to know that you could go to bed at 7 am and then be fresh in a couple of hours time. I just can't do it, I can't fucking do it any more.

AARON *shakes and then sinks his head into his hands.*

RADIO: 'And she's buying a stairway to heaven'.

6 hrs

    AARON stands up and taps the camera.

AARON: The FBI is recording everything we say.

    AARON shouts directly into the camera mic.

AARON: We want to stop the Iraq war right now. George Bush is an asshole.

    AARON picks up his guitar.

AARON: Oh, I've got to sing this before I go to bed.

    AARON twangs his guitar and starts singing.

AARON: 'We're all going on a summer holiday …'. Oh, how I love this.

    AARON holds out his cup for more whisky.

AARON: Come on, fill it up.

6 hrs 15 mins

> PIPPA, JEREMY, HAYLEY, AARON *and* ARIA *are seated at a single table.*

AARON: Have you seen the new Johnny Cash film?

> AARON *starts singing.*

AARON: 'I hear the train a'coming, a'coming round the bend … I hung my head and cried …'.

> AARON *throws his head back and wails—people clap.*

> JEREMY *looks out of the window.*

JEREMY: IKEA – I'm going to mark it now, put it on the map.

HAYLEY: That's the fourth time.

> JEREMY *types I, K, E and A into his hand-held GPS unit.*

6 hrs 30 mins

31/03/2006   04 : 08 : 02   39 kph

    ARIA *and* MEECHY *are still talking intensely.*

MEECHY: The chords are achieved by playing together.

ARIA: Rather than being played on the guitar.

MEECHY: One of my main interests has always been drums.

ARIA: African music is for you.

MEECHY: No, actually, Chinese and all the bashing to scare away spirits.

    ARIA *sees IKEA.*

ARIA: IKEA again. This is like the fifth time we have passed IKEA, so are we going up and down the same road?

JEREMY: At the moment, yeah.

    ARIA *is agitated—he starts to whine.*

ARIA: This is not right. I thought we were going on a much bigger kind of system than going from one side of Milton Keynes to another. Seems we are just in Central Milton Keynes and not in Bletchley.

    *Int/ext—pov shot—*ARIA *turns to look out of the window—it has been raining and the road is wet.*

6 hrs 45 mins

AARON, ARIA, ARCHIE, PIPPA, JEREMY and MEECHY are all seated at the front of the coach—people are beginning to get tired—AARON and ARIA are both drunk—they laugh about the drawing competition they are planning.

AARON: Let's all draw each other with really horrible features.

ARIA: Can you believe he said that? *No* way!

AARON: Have you got a pen?

ARCHIE holds out a handful of pens.

ARCHIE: Red or blue?

PIPPA: I'll have red. Thank you.

The bus swings round a corner—an open bottle of wine wobbles and almost falls over.

MEECHY: Woooo, Jesus. That nearly went everywhere.

AARON looks at his watch.

AARON: This is an art competition, right? Ten minutes to draw the most horrifying image starting … from now.

MEECHY raises his eyebrows.

MEECHY: This might age you.

7 hrs

*They all continue to draw in silence—*MEECHY *interrupts.*

MEECHY: That is really shit, Aria.

ARIA: It is the most horrible thing you could draw …

JEREMY: That's time enough. So how do we judge this?

MEECHY *points at* PIPPA'S *drawing.*

MEECHY: Hers is bloody horrible. (*To* PIPPA.) What do you mean you can't draw?

We see PIPPA'S *drawing—voices continue os.*

JEREMY: His face is over there. That's wrong.

PIPPA: Why is that wrong?

We see MEECHY'S *face lit from below as if in a horror movie.*

MEECHY: So, whose is the most horriblist? I think the red one.

7 hrs 15 mins

ARCHIE *leaves the group.*

Os—rustling noises—a cup falls on the floor.

ARIA: Does anyone have any complaints if I smoke?

MEECHY: As a non-smoker …

ARIA: Will somebody else light up?

PIPPA: I'm not that brave.

ARIA: Then I'll just start drinking again. Hey, as far as I am concerned, these are exceptional circumstances. We can party for forty hours.

AARON *stands up and leaves the group.*

7 hrs 30 mins

AARON *wobbles down the aisle to the back of the coach—he passes* LUCY *as she sleeps sitting up—*ARCHIE *lies asleep with his legs sticking out into the aisle—*AARON *stumbles over* ARCHIE'S *legs before looking at* HAYLEY *curled up, asleep on a seat—at the back of the coach* EDNA *lies across the back seat in her sleeping bag—*AARON *sees the effigy, leans over and rips its head off—he goes to his own seat where he lies down, using the effigy head for his pillow.*

The coach is quiet—the only thing that can be heard is the rattle of the coach interior.

7 hrs 45 mins

31/03/2006   05:23:01   35 kph

MEECHY *looks out of the window.*

MEECHY: The daffodils are out.

ARIA: I'm so bored. Look, Toys R Us!

MEECHY *gets up to leave.*

MEECHY: I am going to go and stretch out a bit.

ARIA *strums the guitar and sings quietly.*

PIPPA *and* ARIA *are the only two* PARTICIPANTS *that remain awake—*PIPPA *faces forward—her demeanor is impassive and neutral as she watches the road ahead of her.*

31/03/2006   05:38:05   37 kph

Int/ext—road—it is raining and the windscreen wipers are on.

Music over: 'That Lonesome Road'.

8 hrs 15 mins

PIPPA *speaks to* ARIA *softly.*

PIPPA: I was just thinking, everyone is asleep.

Int/ext—road—cars with their lights on travel in the opposite direction.

TONY *stops the coach and puts the handbrake on—the coach door opens and we hear the sound of birds singing the dawn chorus.*

8 hrs 30 mins

The new driver, MARK, *gets on the coach—he is bright and wide awake—*TONY *says goodbye and leaves.*

ARIA: Are you our new driver? What's your name?

MARK: Mark.

MARK *and* JEREMY *huddle over the GPS handset—they are engrossed in the map of Milton Keynes.*

MARK: This is mental! It's all of Milton Keynes?

HAYLEY *points at the screen.*

HAYLEY: Look at all the gaps there.

ARCHIE: It is like a bit of lace.

MARK *turns and walks toward the driver's seat—he sits down and starts the engine.*

MARK: I'll try and do the bits where you haven't been.

Lucy's Diary
6:15 am: We've stopped to swap drivers. It feels weird to be still!

31/03/2006   06:23:25   44 kph

> ARIA *continues to strum the guitar quietly—both his playing and the sound of the radio can be heard at the same time.*

RADIO: ... Rain on and off all day.

> PIPPA *remains still, staring into the distance—she is joined by* AARON, ARIA *and* HAYLEY—AARON *breaks the silence.*

AARON: Tomorrow ...

PIPPA: It is tomorrow.

ARIA: Wow, where are we?

> ARIA *looks out of the window—it is early morning and the light outside has a cool blue hue to it.*

9 hrs

31/03/2006   06:38:55   25 kph

A person in a Sinclair C5 cycles past in the opposite direction.

RADIO: MK Horizon Radio 103.3 FM. Good morning. It's Trevor and Ros. It is going to be quite a wet weekend.

MARK *is wearing a Bluetooth earpiece and is speaking on the phone.*

MARK: Hello, there is a lorry sitting right on the Bradfield Roundabout. H2 is it? Doesn't seem to be causing any problems.

RADIO: (*Ros*) It is time for Travel News. Here is the very lovely Stephen.

RADIO: (*Stephen*) I've just spoken to Mark and he says he has just seen a broken-down lorry on the Bradfield Roundabout but it doesn't seem to be causing any major problems at the moment.

RADIO: (*Ros*) Thank you, Steve. You said that Mark called in from New City Coaches. Can you give us an idea what Mark is doing?

RADIO: (*Stephen*) Mark is going to be circling in a bus and driving around MK until about 5 am tomorrow morning.

MARK *turns to* HAYLEY *and smiles.*

MARK: Nice!

9 hrs 15 mins

JEREMY: You haven't been around any roundabouts yet?

MARK: Roundabouts – what are they?

JEREMY: They are roads that last forever.

RADIO: Here are The Beach Boys with 'I Get Around'. It's ten to seven.

MARK: I'll do two roundabouts in a row, then you will have a set of wheels.

RADIO: 'I get around'.

   JEREMY *watches the* GPS *drawing as it is being made.*

JEREMY: Yeah, we can draw handlebars on it. I have done this with cars before, but never a coach.

RADIO: 'Get around, round, round, I get around'.

   ARIA *approaches.*

ARIA: Why are we doing this? Hey, do you know where we are stopping for breakfast?

RADIO: 'Wah wa ooo'.

9 hrs 30 mins

31/03/2006   07:08:00   56 kph

The rest of the PARTICIPANTS *are just beginning to wake up—*
they move slowly around the coach.

MARK: Each area has its own unique housing and its own name.
A lot of it relates. In Pennyland, when we get up to the centre,
you have Shilling Close and it is all Sovereign Drive and all those
sorts of things.

JEREMY: It is still not as rigid as some places in the States.

MARK: Here it is 'H' and 'V', but still fairly twisted.

Int/ext—the road is seen stretching out into the distance.

RADIO: A fairly quiet morning in Milton Keynes. One of our
phone rangers, Mark, called in earlier about a lorry on the
Bradfield Roundabout.

JEREMY: The Bradfield Roundabout – let's head there!

MARK *grins.*

MARK: That was me, I called in earlier. The lorry will probably
be gone now.

9 hrs 45 mins

9 *EXT SERVICE STATION—EARLY MORNING.*

ARIA *gives the camera the finger as the* PARTICIPANTS *get off the coach—*ARIA, AARON *and* LUCY *gather in front of the coach—the sound of the motorway can be heard in the background.*

HAYLEY *and* PIPPA *carry wash bags and go into the service station toilets to wash.*

10 *INT COACH.*

HAYLEY, PIPPA, ARIA, AARON, LUCY *and* ARCHIE *are finding their seats.*

Music over: 'Hit the Road Jack'.

MEECHY *has just woken up and is wiping the sleep from his eyes—*AARON *has gone to lie down again—*EDNA *rubs cream into her hands.*

10 hrs

The coach is messy and people's belongings are scattered over its chairs and tables.

PIPPA *gets up to make a cup of coffee.*

RADIO: The doors of Bletchley Park re-open to the public today after a six-month revamp. The park attracts over forty thousand visitors a year that are fans of Winston Churchill, who want to find out more about what happened in the Second World War.

10 hrs 15 mins

31/03/2006   07:53:13   23 kph

*PIPPA brings two cups of coffee with her to the front of
the bus—ARIA and PIPPA continue their conversation while
drinking coffee.*

ARIA: I saw him last year as well at the Reading Festival – he is
what it should be. There is no force of nature like him. Really
sexy at the same time.

*The sound of an elephant call on the radio interrupts ARIA'S
speech.*

ARIA: He is really awesome and Yoko Ono is great.

PIPPA: She is amazing – must have had a load of surgery.

10 hrs 30 mins

31/03/2006   08:08:00   45 kph

Int/ext—The Point Cinema can be seen from the window— voices continue os.

MARK: The Point is easyCinema.com now. It starts at 50p.

JEREMY: Is it popular?

MARK: I don't know. The Point used to be at the central point of Milton Keynes. When I was growing up, about twenty years ago, that was the place to be with bars and a cinema and that.

HAYLEY: I spent my eighteenth birthday there. I'd been ice-skating and had concussion from falling over. I was watching a spoof horror film, had to go to the loo, got confused and went back into the wrong cinema and ended up watching *Platoon*.

Int/ext—road—the coach is being driven east along Midsummer Boulevard—the sun can be seen rising on the horizon at the end of the road.

ARIA: Ahh, yes! The sunrise.

Light falls on ARIA's face—after ten and a half hours on the coach he now has the beginnings of a beard.

10 hrs 45 mins

RADIO: Horizon Traffic and Travel with IKEA. Cooked breakfast for only 95p.

 HAYLEY *and* JEREMY *talk.*

JEREMY: What about this Gurdjieff?

 HAYLEY'S *hair is ruffled and her make-up is smudged.*

HAYLEY: He was an esoteric teacher who went out driving with some friends and passed a petrol station without filling up his car. His friends wanted him to stop, but he carried on until the car ran out of petrol. This event became part of Gurdjieff's mythology and teachings. I originally planned the bus trip as a critical re-enactment that would ask questions about the journey/life metaphor in his action. I then found many other examples of the metaphor and started thinking about the Road Movie genre, which seemed more relevant to Milton Keynes and its American-style roads. *MKVH* draws on the narrative structures of road movies as well as the Gurdjieff story. East to west and north to south: *MKVH (Milton Keynes Vertical and Horizontal)*.

 Int/ext—hedgerows.

MARK: This is one of the villages that Milton Keynes swallowed up.

JEREMY: This looks out of place in the middle of a big city. I had no idea how big Milton Keynes was.

MARK: It is only half the size. Another twenty years to go yet.

11 hrs

Int/ext—road.

The coach is at a roundabout—a learner driver has stalled in front of the coach—speech continues os.

MARK: Go! Go! Go!

MARK flashes the learner driver with the coach lights.

HAYLEY: Poor thing is probably panicking.

MARK: Ready, steady, go! No, not now, no!

JEREMY: Let's follow him, hound him, for the next thirty minutes.

HAYLEY: It took me five attempts to pass my test.

MARK: I passed my test on Friday the thirteenth after thirteen lessons.

The coach stops at a second roundabout and remains behind the learner driver.

MARK'S face is in a grimace.

MARK: We're back!

JEREMY: Go! Go! Go!

MARK: Oh look, I've stalled now.

MARK restarts the engine—the learner drives off into the distance.

11 hrs 15 mins

HAYLEY *is seated behind* MARK.

HAYLEY: I have arranged to go to Newport Pagnell for breakfast.

MARK: Are they doing a live broadcast from there?

HAYLEY: Supposed to be.

ARIA *joins them.*

ARIA: So you decide on the route?

MARK: What route? When I get somewhere, I just decide where to go from there.

ARIA *looks out of the window—he is distracted for a moment.*

ARIA: Dog walker …

ARIA *turns to address* HAYLEY *directly.*

ARIA: I honestly don't want to go up and down the same stretch of road for hours. I want to see places I haven't seen before.

HAYLEY *pauses.*

HAYLEY: Tony was driving conceptually last night.

ARIA: Conceptually you might say, but you were asleep for most of the time.

11 hrs 30 mins

31/03/2006   09:08:02   16 kph

MARK: I'm just wondering about booking food for tonight?
I'll ring Diane and see if she knows anywhere.

HAYLEY *sees a single magpie at the roadside.*

HAYLEY: (*To herself and in a whisper.*) Hello, Mr Magpie. I hope
your wife and children are fine.

MEECHY *sits down next to* ARIA—MEECHY *is agitated.*

MEECHY: Other people say, 'I'm vegetarian, but I eat fish.'

ARIA: Are you sure about that?

MEECHY: Vegetarians can't eat fish. Vegans can't eat dairy
products.

ARIA *spots* JUSTIN *from the coach window.*

ARIA: Justin?

The coach stops.

11 hrs 45 mins

*11 EXT NEWPORT PAGNELL SERVICES—
CAR PARK.*

MICHAEL STANLEY *and the radio* INTERVIEWER *are waiting
for the coach in the car park of Newport Pagnell Services—
it is sunny.*

MICHAEL: How's it going?

HAYLEY, JEREMY *and* MARK *stand next to the coach and
introduce themselves to the* INTERVIEWER—JUSTIN *arrives
and stands to the left of the group—he is videoing the interview
with his hand-held camera.*

The INTERVIEWER *has a large microphone—he is wearing
an earpiece.*

INTERVIEWER: So, basically what will happen is that the
presenter, George, will throw it over to me.

HAYLEY: So it is like an update?

INTERVIEWER: Pretty much, yeah.

Background noise as GEORGE *starts to introduce the interview
on radio.*

INTERVIEWER: Good morning George. Well I haven't been
inside it, but I have just caught it as it is taking one of its breaks,
and I am joined now by … oh, dodgy signal.

The radio signal breaks down—a mobile phone rings and the
INTERVIEWER *answers it.*

INTERVIEWER: Hello? Hello Becky.

The INTERVIEWER *starts conducting the interview over his mobile phone.*

INTERVIEWER: As I was trying to say before, I have not been inside the coach, but I have just caught them on their break as they have been going around Milton Keynes on this artwork. I am joined now by three people who have been on the coach: Mark the driver, June Newson who has been involved with the project and had the conception for it and Jeremy Wood who has been on the coach doing some GPS drawings on there. Good morning to you all. Mark, first of all, the coach has been going around. How much petrol is left?

MARK: I think we have done about a third of the tank in 250 miles, so in my estimation, another twenty-four hours.

INTERVIEWER: Another twenty-four hours in there?

MARK: Yes, I am afraid so.

INTERVIEWER: And are you going to be driving for all that time as well?

MARK: No, because the law doesn't allow us to. But I will be driving until lunchtime, there will be another driver on from teatime 'til about midnight, then another driver from then until it runs out, hopefully.

12 hrs

INTERVIEWER: Ok, thank you very much. Right. Now Hayley, you were involved with the whole idea of this. First of all, explain why you came up with this idea and where it came from?

HAYLEY: Well, I wanted to make an artwork that wasn't just about hanging something on the walls but something that really activated discussion. So I came up with this idea that was a journey and a journey is like a story, and it is lots of people's stories. There are lots of different ideas of what it is, so it is quite open.

INTERVIEWER: And what has it been like inside the coach? You have been in there since nine o'clock last night, and you have got another twenty-four hours to go, so what has the atmosphere been like inside the coach?

HAYLEY: It has been very funny. There was guitar playing and singing last night. Some people stayed up all night and watched the sunrise. Other people have been able to sleep. So it has been very mixed. It is probably getting a bit smelly in there now though.

INTERVIEWER: Thank you very much. Now Jeremy, you have been sitting in the coach as well, doing some GPS drawings in there. Can you just explain to me what that is all about and why you are doing that?

JEREMY: Right, the GPS drawing is to trace the route of the bus that has been taken and to make a map at the end of the entire route and see where it has been.

INTERVIEWER: And how has it been for you inside there? You have been in there with all the other people, with Hayley and the driver.

JEREMY: It's been funnier than I expected. I didn't expect people to be so jovial. It has been good. Sleep hasn't been that easy, but we're getting by, we're getting by.

INTERVIEWER: That's great, thank you very much. That was Jeremy, Hayley and Mark who are on this bus. As you were hearing there it has got another twenty-four hours to go, so maybe we will be able to catch up with it later on. Back to you two in the studio, George.

12 hrs 15 mins

12 INT NEWPORT PAGNELL SERVICES—
CANTEEN.

EDNA *and* PIPPA *are queuing for food—*PIPPA *puts food on her plate and* EDNA *takes out her purse—they are both joking and laughing.*

JUSTIN *is videoing* EDNA *and* PIPPA*—he is approached by the* SERVICE STATION MANAGER.

MANAGER: Excuse me mate, what are you actually filming there?

JUSTIN *points to* EDNA *and* PIPPA.

JUSTIN: These two … there, in the middle.

This explanation satisfies the SERVICE STATION MANAGER*—* JUSTIN *continues videoing.*

31/03/2006   10: 08: 04   0. 71 kph

> ARCHIE, HAYLEY *and* MICHAEL *are sat eating breakfast—
> each is eating a different combination of the following: hash
> browns with egg, beans, tomatoes and mushrooms.*

MICHAEL: So where are you from?

ARCHIE: Towcester/Silverstone round there.

MICHAEL: Oh that is good. I live in Paulerspury.

ARCHIE: Oh really, I used to go to school there.

MICHAEL: That is where my little boy goes.

ARCHIE: My dad did the garden there – the playground.

> MICHAEL *turns to* HAYLEY.

MICHAEL: Did you hear me beep you last night? I overtook
the coach on the way home. I'll give you a ring later to see how
things are going. Meantime, give me a call if you need to.

> MICHAEL *says goodbye to everyone and leaves.*

12 hrs 45 mins

31/03/2006   10:23:04   34 kph

    13 EXT NEWPORT PAGNELL SERVICES—
CAR PARK.

    HAYLEY *and* JUSTIN *stand talking.*

JUSTIN: Ok, so I'll see you there in twenty minutes.

    HAYLEY *gets on the coach.*

    Music over: 'Penny Lane'.

    14 INT JUSTIN'S CAR.

    JUSTIN *videos the coach with a hand-held camera—he follows the coach as it is driven out of shot.*

    JUSTIN *continues to follow the coach by car—it is a bright day.*

    The camera picks out the following road names:

    V7 Saxon Street
    H4 Dansteed Way
    V4 Watling Street
    H7 Childs Way

    Music fades out.

RADIO: The man that is in charge of the pleasure boat that has capsised in Bahrain killing at least fifty-seven people is still being questioned this morning.

13 hrs

15 INT COACH.

RADIO: Investigators are looking to see if there were too many people on board. The man at the helm wasn't even the captain.

HAYLEY *sits on the steps at the front of the coach.*

HAYLEY: Your driving style is nice, very gentle.

MARK'S *phone rings—he answers it.*

MARK: Where was it, Diane? The Talbot at Loughton. Can you book dinner for ten people at 7:30 pm? I'm near Loughton now. We'll head over there.

RADIO: Naomi Campbell is accused of throwing a mobile phone at her housekeeper.

MARK: Big news. That will wake everyone up.

HAYLEY *talks with* JUSTIN *on her mobile.*

HAYLEY: We are just checking out where we are going to eat later.

Int/ext—road.

JEREMY: The roads are getting thinner and thinner.

The Talbot pub is in shot.

MARK: There it is.

13 hrs 15 mins

31/03/2006   10:53:17   26 kph

HAYLEY: We need to find Justin.

*Int/ext—road—the sun is bright and the street lights cast long shadows on the ground—*MARK *suddenly spots* JUSTIN.

MARK: There he is. He has even put cones out!

JUSTIN *is parked in a lay-by surrounded by building works— he videos the coach as it is being driven past.*

JUSTIN *gets in his car and follows the coach.*

13 hrs 30 mins

31/03/2006   11:08:01   68 kph

EDNA is recounting stories about Milton Keynes.

EDNA: Do go down to Caldecott Business Park. I think this business park is a model of excellence. I often bring people down here.

JEREMY: You also have to give us a tour of your home.

EDNA smiles and she becomes more animated.

EDNA: Do you want to go there? It was one of the first houses the district council built in the early seventies to house the first architects, because there was nowhere for people to live.

Int/ext—road—there is blossom on the trees—people ride along adjacent cycling paths.

Conversation continues os.

EDNA: We turn left here.

HAYLEY: Ahh, that is Tinkers Bridge.

EDNA: It is one of the saddest, most run-down estates in Milton Keynes, so at least it can only get better. (*To* MARK.) Keep going to the end and you will be able to turn around.

The road gets narrower.

EDNA: (*Pointing.*) This one is mine.

The coach stops outside EDNA's house.

JEREMY: I thought there was space to turn around here?

MARK: It would be alright if I was in a Mini!

The coach is now trapped in a small cul-de-sac—MARK *turns the coach around by slowly inching it backward and forward.*

16 EXT MARSHWORTH CUL-DE-SAC.

LUCY *stands on the kerb next to the coach.*

LUCY: Let's go and play on the swings.

LUCY, ARIA *and* ARCHIE *run up the hill to the playground—* EDNA, PIPPA, MEECHY, HAYLEY *and* JEREMY *walk towards* EDNA'S *house.*

31/03/2006   11:23:05   0.26 kph

17 INT EDNA'S HOUSE.

HAYLEY, PIPPA, MEECHY *and* JEREMY *walk around* EDNA'S *house—her voice is heard os.*

EDNA: I found we had turned into Marshworth (where I am living), a quiet cul-de-sac off Groveway, the busy east-west highway just north of Bletchley. This comprises the first twenty-four properties built by the Milton Keynes Development Corporation to house their first architects and planners, for in the Buckinghamshire agricultural land of the seventies, there was nowhere for them to live.

This is now considered probably the best-designed estate, and my house, which has remained single storey and retains all its original features, is much admired. So many have been changed by the addition of second floors and gable roofs.

I asked if my fellow travellers would like to have a look, and there was a general consensus. It is a one storey, very spacious accommodation with twelve rooms, a garage, lockup carport and a small garden with a vista of the Grand Union Canal and its passing boats, the grounds of the Open University and a small farm. It is hard to believe one is inside a city. My lodger has their own sitting room, bedroom and shower room. We share the kitchen and I have the rest which includes a wonderful studio and library/office.

The dawns are beautiful, rising from the Lombardy poplars; the garden full of birds; and the sun fills the floor to ceiling windows all day. Lucky me.

14 hrs

18 INT COACH.

*The coach is parked—*MARK *is speaking on his mobile phone—*
he is being interviewed by Horizon Radio.

MARK: Once they joined the coach on Thursday evening, that
was it, they couldn't get off.

MARK *pauses as he listens to a question.*

MARK: It is everywhere. The first driver stuck to the grid. I am
trying to take it off into areas where I can still take the coach, so
the white New City Coach you see driving round Milton Keynes
is the 'art coach'. One of the people of the coach has been
playing the guitar during the night to keep their spirits up. They
have been sleeping through the day and are awake during the
night, which is good for the drivers. Oh, it has certainly changed
my life …

MEECHY: (*Singing.*) 'Roll-up for the Mystery Tour …'.

MARK: All in the name of art, that is what they say. Cheers Ros.
Bye Cueball.

14 hrs 15 mins

MARK *starts the coach engine and begins driving.*

ARCHIE *and* LUCY *are bored—they are looking for things to do.*

ARCHIE: So, what movies do we have?

LUCY: *Bonnie and Clyde*; *Road to Perdition*; *Thelma and Louise*; *Pow Wow Highway*; *Vanishing Point*; *Convoy*; *The Wild Angels*; *Speed*; *Broken Flowers*; *The Road to Guantánamo*; *The Adventures of Priscilla, Queen of the Desert*; *Road to Morocco*; *Stranger than Paradise*; *A Tout de Suite*; *Adventures of Felix*; *Detour*; *Exiles*; *Get on the Bus*; *Freeway*; *Grand Voyage*; *It Happened One Night*; *Hard Drive*; *The Blues Brothers*; *Kalifornia*; *Two Lane Blacktop*; *The Getaway*; *Guantanamera*; *Bound for Glory*; *Alice Doesn't Live Here Anymore*; *The Wild One*; *Rebel Without a Cause*; *Dear Diary*; *Close to Eden*; *They Drive by Night*; *The Wizard of Oz*; *The Gleaners and I*; *Down by Law*; *Drugstore Cowboy*; *Easy Rider*; *Y Tu Mamá También*; *In July*; *Hells Angels on Wheels*; *Sideways*; *Fear and Loathing in Las Vegas*; *Transamerica*; *In This World*; *Another Day in Paradise*; *Smoke Signals*; *The Grapes of Wrath*; *The Last Detail*; *Kings of the Road*; *Hell's Belles*; *Red Salute*; *Stagecoach*; *Lolita*; *My Own Private Idaho*; *Paris, Texas*; *Desperate*; *The Hitchhiker*; *O Brother, Where Art Thou?*; *Vagabond*; *The Living End*; *The Motorcycle Diaries*; *Ariel*; *Natural Born Killers*; *Alice In The Cities*; *The Road Warrior*; *The Sugarland Express*; *Sullivan's Travels*; *Thieves Like Us*; *True Romance*; *Two for the Road*; *Badlands*; *The Milky Way* …

14 hrs 30 mins

31/03/2006   12:08:01   45 kph

The coach is being driven round a roundabout.

Music over: 'The Long and Winding Road'.

PIPPA, ARIA *and* HAYLEY *are sat together—they are mainly silent and only speak occasionally.*

PIPPA: (*To* MARK.) What are you going to have? Black coffee? I'll have a black coffee as well. Let's do it.

PIPPA *stands up.*

HAYLEY: Well, we are off our map already.

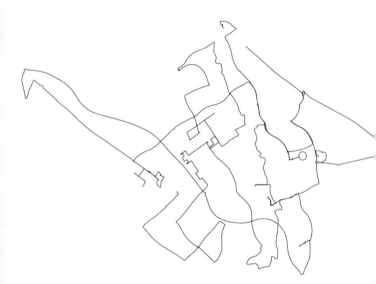

14 hrs 45 mins

MARK: We are in Stony Stratford, the old A5. It is an old Roman Road. It will take you all the way from London to Wales.

Music fades out—general ad lib talking.

ARIA: There are very funny things like *Shameless*.

PIPPA: I love *Shameless*.

ARIA: My mother and I were watching it together. We couldn't stop laughing for half an hour.

Silence.

RADIO: Sunny spells amongst the clouds today.

HAYLEY: (*To* ARIA.) Can you pass me that bag of sandwiches? We are going to eat them in Campbell Park.

The coach stops.

15 hrs

19 EXT CAMPBELL PARK.

The weather is changeable—bright/dull/cool/windy—daffodils blow in the wind and the pond surface is choppy.

JEREMY has his hand-held GPS unit with him.

ARCHIE: Can I do a GPS drawing in the park?

JEREMY: Yes, but I don't think it will register.

JEREMY gives ARCHIE his hand-held GPS unit.

ARCHIE takes off his jacket and runs across the park and along the horizon before zigzagging back across the field towards JEREMY.

15 hrs 15 mins

*There is a bag of sandwiches on the bench—*HAYLEY *arranges the sandwiches in a neat line on the edge of the bench.*

HAYLEY: (*To* EDNA.) Would you like to sit down?

EDNA *sits down—she opens a sandwich packet and begins to eat.*

MEECHY *and* ARIA *stand on the small bridge talking.*

JEREMY *rolls a cigarette.*

LUCY *rubs her arms to keep warm.*

PIPPA *sits next to* EDNA *and eats a sandwich.*

15 hrs 30 mins

31/03/2006   13:08:14   0.07 kph

    20 INT COACH.

    MARK *is packing his bag as* IAN *gets on the coach.*

MARK: Bye, see you later!

    IAN *starts engine and the coach pulls away.*

RADIO: In the meantime we have 'These Boots are Made for Walkin'' by Nancy Sinatra.

15 hrs 45 mins

31/03/2006   13 : 23 : 02   56 kph

HAYLEY *turns her head to the left and looks out of the window.*

Int/ext—flash cuts of buildings—the bus is seen reflected in large glass windows as it passes by—Milton Keynes is busy with cars, buses and pedestrians.

Radio: 'Are you ready, boots? Start walkin'.'

Conversation continues os.

ARIA: That is the Hockey Stadium, but they have football games there. The problem is that the glass bounces the sound around and it has terrible acoustics.

PIPPA: If we pass IKEA, wake me up, stamp on me.

RADIO: Milton Keynes 103.3 FM.

16 hrs

*The coach is in Bletchley—*ARIA *and* PIPPA *look out of the window—they are straining to see something.*

ARIA: The side of it where the rail tracks are. You can really see the sun shining through.

PIPPA: Is it that place you were talking about?

ARIA: Yes, that's the place and I think there was actually vegetation. Yeah, that is the place. There is not really much else in the centre, there is a huge Tesco and a train station.

Int/ext—view of the high street—there is a glimpse of a church spire.

ARIA: Redrum, redrum. There are a few graveyards in Stony Stratford. My favourite is near the station. (*Pointing.*) That's the Fox and Hounds. On your left, there is a graveyard.

16 hrs 15 mins

Int/ext—road.

The surrounding area begins to change from being a relatively built-up environment to a rural one—pavement becomes grass verge.

HAYLEY *looks at the GPS device.*

HAYLEY: This is interesting. Are we going right round the outside of Milton Keynes?

*It starts raining—*IAN *turns the windscreen wipers on.*

ARIA: Grrrrrr.

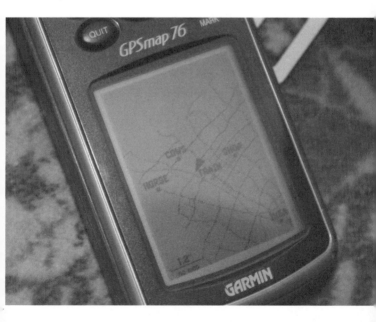

16 hrs 30 mins

The coach slows down and a rainbow is seen in an adjacent field.

The camera focuses on raindrops trickling down the windowpane—the sound of water under the coach wheels can be heard.

RADIO: For all you drivers out there in the rain, here is Tom Waits with 'Diamonds on my Windshield'.

HAYLEY: (*Os.*) What do you think about taking this job on?

RADIO: 'Diamonds on my windshield, tears from heaven, pulling into town on the Interstate'.

The sound of rain gets heavier and starts drowning out the speech.

IAN: To be honest, I would take anything on.

HAYLEY: That is very pragmatic of you.

HAYLEY *looks out the window—she talks at random.*

HAYLEY: It looks like Netherfield here.

RADIO: 'The eights go east and the fives go north, and the merging nexus back and forth'.

The rain gets even heavier.

16 hrs 45 mins

31/03/2006   14:23:02   58 kph

IAN: This is Lakeside. I used to live here many years ago.
The only place I could get was next to the London Pride pub.
It was a nightmare.

HAYLEY: So you are the one that is going to pump the engine.
Are you going to do it where the coach stops, on site?

IAN: Yes. Shame about the weather.

HAYLEY: I've always thought that driving in the rain was
quite nice.

It starts hailing.

17 hrs

HAYLEY'S mobile phone rings—the name 'Robin' flashes up on its screen—HAYLEY answers.

HAYLEY: Hi Robin! It's all going very well. We have got through half a tank and I think we might be going until about 11am tomorrow.

She listens.

HAYLEY: Yeah, it is intimate, but people have got space to move around.

She listens.

HAYLEY: Aaron got very drunk last night and was singing. He's been sleeping all day. We are going through tired bits and grottiness. Mark the driver was doing traffic reports this morning. Yes, I'll give you a ring next week. Bye.

IAN shouts back to HAYLEY.

IAN: We have been going for nearly one hour thirty minutes Hayley. Do you want a break?

HAYLEY: Only if you do.

IAN: I could do with going to the toilet. Best bet is to go back over to Kingston. I'm sure McDonald's won't mind us using their toilet, everybody else does.

17 hrs 15 mins

31/03/2006   14:53:03   0.58 kph

21 EXT ROADSIDE.

AARON *stumbles off the coach—he looks dazed.*

JEREMY: You slept all day!

AARON: I don't know how I did it. How long until food?

JEREMY: It was a very long night.

AARON *goes back to his seat and looks out of the window— everything is still—*MEECHY *reads.*

The others get silently back onto the coach—they are wet from the rain.

22 INT COACH.

IAN *turns the ignition on and the coach engine starts.*

17 hrs 30 mins

31/03/2006   15:08:05   66 kph

17 hrs 45 mins

31/03/2006   15:23:00   67 kph

18 hrs

EDNA: Can we stop at Central Station?

IAN: Why?

EDNA: Because I couldn't find an *Evening Standard* when we stopped.

IAN: We could loop round that way, yes.

> IAN *is arranging the next shift on his phone.*

IAN: Fred, when are you coming out?

> IAN *scratches his head.*

IAN: Do you have dinner plans? Because they are going for dinner at 7:30. You just ring me when you are ready to come out and I'll pick you up. I'll speak to you later.

> *The coach is quiet again*—AARON *continues to lie in a foetal position with his head covered*—ARCHIE *is listening to music*—EDNA *is reading a book*—MEECHY *looks tired as he drifts in and out of sleep*—HAYLEY *moves around the coach aimlessly.*

18 hrs 15 mins

31/03/2006   15:53:01   63 kph

PIPPA, LUCY *and* JEREMY *sit reading the* MK News.

PIPPA: I just want to read the letters page.

'SIR – Regarding the article on the commissioning of a piece of live art by the Milton Keynes Gallery. I read the article with incredulous disbelief. The artist Hayley Newman, however talented, appears a young lady who displays both a high degree of naïvety and a total lack of artistic understanding, a glowing ability to waste money. If our 'artist' is so curious to find the outcome when a bus runs out of petrol, I suggest that she returns to the real world and takes a journey with the MK Metro, the local bus service provider. Lack of diesel and other mechanical failings is not an everyday, but hourly occurrence for the long-suffering travelling public. I doubt they find anything remotely artistic in waiting in a lay-by in Saxon Street, while an engineer comes along in a battered old van and 'pumps the engine' before the journey can continue. This whole exercise is a waste of money and an insult to the public who have to use the buses in Milton Keynes. Rather than highlight the misery, in some form of art, Hayley Newman would be best advised to direct her talents elsewhere. If she would like to 'rest her brushes' I can retell some very artistic stories and paint some extremely vivid pictures of passenger reactions when my bus runs out of diesel or suffers mechanical breakdown on a busy grid road and we wait over half an hour to be rescued by a well-meaning engineer with a jerry can of fuel. The cost of my artistic views of an everyday occurrence on the buses to Hayley Newman? Nothing. I will provide my artistic services of the real world completely free of charge. The finished article can be in oils, pastels or crayons, it does not really matter.
MK Metro Driver'.

18 hrs 30 mins

31/03/2006   16:08:04   0.17 kph

The speedometer shows the coach slowing down.

*The coach stops—*EDNA *gets off the coach to buy a copy of the* Evening Standard.

HAYLEY *smiles and whispers in* PIPPA'S *ear.*

HAYLEY: Let's make sure that no one gets off or on, otherwise we will be here forever.

Two boys point at the effigy, they stare and laugh.

PIPPA: Those two guys have seen the body.

The EFFIGY'S *head has been put back on its body.*

HAYLEY'S *phone beeps.*

HAYLEY: Ian, I have just had a text from Justin to ask if you can go past Campbell Park. He must be waiting there with his video camera.

Lucy's Diary
4:15 pm: This is turning into a bit of a marathon. God knows when I will get home.

18 hrs 45 mins

31/03/2006   16: 23: 03   48 kph

*The speedometer shows the coach speeding up—*IAN *points out* JUSTIN*—he is standing at the edge of the road videoing the coach as it passes by.*

IAN: There he is, over there.

HAYLEY: He is undercover. Don't look him in the eye, he'll hypnotise you.

23   EXT LAY-BY.

*Pov—*JUSTIN *follows the coach until it drives out of shot.*

19 hrs

24 INT JUSTIN'S CAR.

JUSTIN'S *windscreen wipers squeak—the car is messy and there are newspapers and sweet wrappers on the passenger seat.*

RADIO: Think, don't drink and drive.

JUSTIN'S *phone rings—he answers it.*

JUSTIN: Hi Hayley. How many miles have I done? Let me check.

JUSTIN *checks his milometer.*

JUSTIN: I've clocked over sixty following you today. You must have done over a thousand.

*The coach comes into view—*JUSTIN *starts his car and follows the coach.*

19 hrs 15 mins

JUSTIN *indicates right to overtake the coach—*MEECHY *and* ARCHIE *can be seen looking out of the coach window—they are staring into the distance and don't see* JUSTIN *as he drives by.*

We see a signpost that reads 'Walton's Wood'.

JUSTIN *indicates and parks in a lay-by—he videos the coach as it passes by—he starts his car and continues to follow the coach.*

31/03/2006   17: 08: 04   57 kph

25 INT COACH.

ARCHIE, ARIA, MEECHY *and* PIPPA *are seated—their speech is barely audible as the noise from the coach engine drowns it out.*

MEECHY: Polished.

ARCHIE: He never felt like …

MEECHY: When I was in London, and the, erm …

LUCY *looks out of the window—the sun is low in the sky.*

MEECHY: I can't remember it, I haven't been there since. I actually used to sit up trees once.

Bright light reflects off the windowpane.

PIPPA: I was just being quiet more than anything else.

31/03/2006   17:23:17   24 kph

HAYLEY *is reading a newspaper:*

'The Iranian government yesterday brushed aside a thirty-day deadline imposed by the United Nations Security Council to halt its nuclear programme. Ali Asghar Soltanieh, Tehran's chief representative to the International Atomic Energy Agency, the UN nuclear watchdog, said Iran had no intention of co-operating with the latest diplomatic attempt to get it to abandon its enrichment of uranium, which it says is only intended to lead to civilian nuclear power, saying: 'The enrichment matter is not reversible'. The UN Security Council, after weeks of deadlock, finally agreed a statement on Wednesday night calling for suspension of enrichment and setting the deadline'.

20 hrs

PIPPA *is in the middle of telling a long story.*

PIPPA: First thing I do is come in armed with razors, hair removing cream and God knows what else. You shave me, just pluck me, whatever you do.

HAYLEY *looks up from her newspaper.*

HAYLEY: My sister is a trombonist and when she plays her instrument a lot the hair on her top lip goes green from oxidisation. I remember her buying bleach to get rid of it when we were kids.

20 hrs 15 mins

We see MEECHY'S *closed eyes—they are moving rapidly from side to side as he dreams about the trip—conversations come back to him as a series of flashbacks:*

ARIA *is seen impersonating a drum machine and talking about music—his face is lit from below.*

EDNA *talks about how Milton Keynes got its outdoor sculptures—*MEECHY *dreams that the bus has turned into a gigantic soft sculpture.*

JUSTIN *bounces onto the bus—he is wearing full armour and talking about life in Newport Pagnell.*

JEREMY *carries a giant global positioning device—it is twice his size—on it he draws a portrait of* MEECHY.

PIPPA *and* ARCHIE *sit opposite each other and talk about the origin of names.*

MEECHY *imagines the spectre of* LUCY *wearing a football scarf and screaming at the top of her voice.*

MEECHY *is on his knees in front of* TIM'S EFFIGY*—he interviews the* EFFIGY *about life as an art project mascot— the effigy murmurs a reply.*

MEECHY *wakes with a sudden jolt.*

20 hrs 30 mins

31/03/2006   18:08:02   47 kph

Int/ext—road—white stripes on tarmac.

MEECHY *turns to his left and leans over to speak to* LUCY.

MEECHY: If Hayley changes her mind and wants to go to Newport Pagnell, get her to tell me. Pass it on.

LUCY *leans forward and whispers in* ARIA'S *ear.*

LUCY: Meechy says, 'If Hayley changes her mind and wants to go to Newport Pagnell, can she tell him?'

ARIA *leans forward to speak to* HAYLEY.

ARIA: Hayley, Meechy says to tell him if you change your mind about going to Newport Pagnell.

HAYLEY: I will, don't worry.

ARIA *leans back and whispers in* LUCY'S *ear.*

ARIA: She will, don't worry.

LUCY *leans back and speaks to* MEECHY.

LUCY: She will, don't worry.

MEECHY *nods.*

20 hrs 45 mins

Music over: 'Middle of the Road'.

AARON *and* PIPPA *are sat together.*

AARON: Did you ever see the performance like this with Marina and Ulay? When they drove round and round in a little van and documented it? They drove round for 365 laps and gradually a circle of tyre marks appeared on the ground.

Int/ext—window.

HAYLEY: Keeping moving is very compulsive. It is as if I am being mesmerised by the road.

Music fades out.

21 hrs

> *The coach is being driven east-west along Midsummer*
> *Boulevard—the sun is seen setting on the horizon at the*
> *end of the street.*

RADIO: It is just the little things really. Like kicking the ball over
the park with my son, walks with my wife. But with my injuries
I know my problems have only just begun. At Fennemores
Solicitors our job is to get you the accident compensation you
deserve and ensure that you receive a hundred percent of your
claim every time. Get Milton Keynes' leading personal injury
lawyers on your side. Call Fennemores on Milton Keynes
678241.

21 hrs 15 mins

31/03/2006   18:53:06   30 kph

Lucy's Diary
7 pm: There have definitely been points today when I have felt
rather surreal as if I was in a film – one of those road movies.
Looking out of the window was like watching a film screen as
if what was outside wasn't real anymore. Quite strange. I still
haven't wondered what am I doing here but am well and truly
in it now.

21 hrs 30 mins

31/03/2006   19:08:06   30 kph

21 hrs 45 mins

The coach is driven into Milton Keynes Marina—the new driver FRED *stands at the water's edge waiting to be picked up.*

26 EXT MILTON KEYNES MARINA—NIGHT.

The PARTICIPANTS *stand in front of the coach—they are lit by its headlights.*

FRED: Hiya!

IAN: How are you, my boy?

MEECHY: Driver?

ARCHIE: Give him a chance, Meech!

HAYLEY: You want to go and collect you computer from home, don't you?

MEECHY: Yes, if possible please.

22 hrs

27 INT COACH.

Int/ext—road—it is narrow and dark—voices continue os.

HAYLEY: We went to The Talbot to check it out this morning. Now I can't remember the exit. Have we been down here already, Jeremy?

JEREMY *looks at his GPS handset.*

JEREMY: Yes, we have been here before.

HAYLEY: I remember these street bumps.

We hear FRED *trying to get the coach into gear.*

JEREMY: Watch the cars!

The coach swerves.

FRED: Is it the Harvester?

The coach stops outside The Talbot pub.

HAYLEY: Are you coming in with us?

FRED: Yes, I'm just going to sort some bits here.

22 hrs 15 mins

28 INT THE TALBOT CARVERY.

Flash cuts of food and drink—the carvery is much brighter than the bus and everything suddenly seems light and colourful.

Indistinct muzak plays in the background.

JEREMY *is at the bar with* ARCHIE *and* LUCY—*everyone seems relieved to be off the coach.*

JEREMY: Can I get you both a drink?

EDNA, HAYLEY *and* MEECHY *sit at the table—a waitress writes down their order—the others join them one by one.*

22 hrs 30 mins

*The camera pans across the carvery display—a side of beef, roast potatoes, peas, brussel sprouts, gravy, carrots and chicken —before stopping at the Yorkshire pudding—*PIPPA *is helping herself to food—she carves meat and puts vegetables onto her plate.*

FRED, HAYLEY, JEREMY, ARIA, EDNA, MEECHY, LUCY, ARCHIE *and* JUSTIN *are seated at a long table—*PIPPA *joins them.*

AARON *drags on a cigarette.*

JEREMY *pours everyone a glass of wine.*

HAYLEY: A toast to Mystery!

The PARTICIPANTS *all raise their glasses and make a toast.*

ARIA *pours gravy over his food.*

ARIA: It is so good to be still.

EDNA *has a look of contentment on her face as she eats.*

EDNA: The food is great – perfect!

22 hrs 45 mins

31/03/2006   20:23:00   0.37 kph

The tabletop is covered with food and drink.

HAYLEY: Fred, could you take a photo of us all?

HAYLEY hands her digital camera to FRED.

*FRED walks to the end of the table to take the photo—
the PARTICIPANTS pose and look into the camera.*

FRED: Say cheese!

ALL: Cheese!

*The PARTICIPANTS start talking amongst themselves again—
JEREMY stands up.*

JEREMY: Ok, so guys, one more for the road?

23 hrs

29 INT COACH.

FRED *turns and speaks to* HAYLEY.

FRED: Ready when you are Hayley.

FRED *starts the engine.*

HAYLEY: OK, we are off.

ARCHIE *and* MEECHY *read out loud to the group.*

MEECHY: There is a top tip in here: 'Tie everything you own to a single piece of string, if you loose anything, keep pulling along the string until you find it'.

General laughter.

ARCHIE: 'If you are going out for a bicycle ride, take a piece of garlic bread and use it as a comfy cushion. Hey presto, warm snack'.

MEECHY: 'Pretend that there are speed humps down the length of your street by flashing your full beam headlights every few yards'.

23 hrs 15 mins

30 INT JUSTIN'S CAR.

JUSTIN *follows the coach in his car—it is dark—the dashboard of the car is lit up and can be seen in the foreground of the shot.*

The coach brake lights come on—the coach slows down as it approaches a roundabout—it indicates right and takes the third exit and continues to travel along the road—the coach brake lights come on—the coach slows down as it approaches a roundabout—it indicates left and takes the first exit and continues to travel along the road—the coach brake lights come on—the coach slows down as it approaches a roundabout—it indicates right and takes the third exit and continues to travel along the road—the coach brake lights come on—the coach slows down as it approaches a roundabout—the coach takes the second exit and continues to travel along the road—the coach brake lights come on— the coach slows down as it approaches a roundabout—it indicates right and takes the third exit and continues to travel along the road—the coach brake lights come on—the coach slows down as it approaches a roundabout—the coach takes the second exit and continues to travel along the road— JUSTIN *turns left and stops following the coach.*

31/03/2006   21:08:06   38 kph

31 INT COACH.

ARCHIE *is doing a crossword.*

ARCHIE: First down?

JEREMY *frowns.*

JEREMY: Ermm, first down is 'drop'.

LUCY *joins them.*

LUCY: Crosswords!

23 hrs 45 mins

31/03/2006   21:23:13   43 kph

ARCHIE: British title, four letters, ends in an 'a'.

 ARIA *sips wine.*

ARIA: Lady 'a'.

LUCY: Mist 'a'.

ARIA: Small drinks?

ALL: Shots.

ARIA: Brainstorm, four letters.

 ARCHIE *frowns.*

ARCHIE: Think …

 ARIA *looks agitated.*

ARIA: No, it is four letters.

 LUCY *shouts.*

LUCY: Fink! Just put it in.

24 hrs

32 EXT COACH.

Music over: 'Stayin' Alive'.

The coach is shot from varying angles as it drives round the city centre:

The coach passes from right to left and left to right.

The camera trucks behind the coach and then forward alongside the coach.

The camera trucks back and pans left to the verge.

The coach is mirrored in a reflective building as it drives past.

Flash cuts of the city and countryside.

The camera trucks beneath tree branches—the moon shines through them.

31/03/2006   21:53:00   53 kph

FRED *speaks over the coach microphone.*

FRED: Just round the corner – you can see the lights there –
that is the small Tesco store if anyone wants to use it.

Silence.

FRED: No one?

LUCY: Yes, I think someone is going to get some cash.

Sound of rustling os.

AARON *and* ARIA *run across the road, dodging traffic.*

LUCY: They are going cross country.

FRED: I'm not so sure that is the best way.

The coach is quiet—everyone waits for AARON *and* ARIA
to return.

24 hrs 30 mins

AARON *arrives—he holds two bottles in the air.*

AARON: Here we go then.

ARIA *waves a corkscrew in the air.*

ARIA: (*Singing to the tune of 'He's Got the Whole World in his Hands'.*) He's got the cork-screw in his hands!

LUCY *and* ARCHIE *take the bottle opener and sing with it.*

ALL: (*Copying* ARIA.) He's got the cork-screw in his hands!

LUCY *draws everyone's attention back to the crosswords.*

LUCY: German dramatist … Bertolt something, second name, dramatist.

ARIA *puts down his pen.*

ARIA: I will *not* give up.

LUCY *scratches her head.*

LUCY: It makes you crazy!

ARIA: Free like Americas? Begins with 'd'?

LUCY: (*Shouting.*) Dude.

24 hrs 45 mins

31/03/2006 22:23:09 56 kph

The camera dollies from the front to the back of the coach.

The camera passes HAYLEY, ARCHIE, AARON, JEREMY, LUCY *and* ARIA *seated at the front of the coach—it skims over empty seats with belongings strewn all over them—it pans across the coffee-making facilities and an overflowing rubbish bin—* MEECHY *listens to music on a personal stereo and looks out of the window—the camera passes the effigy of* TIM *before reaching the back seat, where* PIPPA *and* EDNA *sit talking.*

25 hrs

The camera rests on LUCY *and* ARIA.

LUCY: You are supposed to be doing that one (LUCY *points to a copy of* The National Enquirer.) because it is American. It is a word that relates to speed.

ARIA: Speed rate?

FRED'S *phone rings—he stops the coach and answers it.*

FRED: Hello, how are you my boy? Where are we going to meet? I'll head back for the BP garage and we should see you there, boss! It is where the V8 crosses the H8. Twelve-thirty!

25 hrs 15 mins

AARON *suddenly becomes aware of the hard disk recorder that is hidden under a seat at the front of the coach.*

AARON: Hayley is making a really long recording. How many hours have you got?

HAYLEY: Thirty-six – my age.

AARON: Jesus, really? What format are you going to store it on? Jeremy, what media is that thing there?

JEREMY: Hard disk.

The LCD monitor on the video camera relays a live feed of the road as the coach is driven around Milton Keynes.

AARON: Can it play back?

JEREMY: Yup. The signal comes straight down from the camera into the recorder. The recorder compresses it into MPEG 2. You could compress it more, so you could create more time. It is amazing what those things can do.

HAYLEY *laughs.*

HAYLEY: Fill up the hard drive and empty the tanks.

Lucy's Diary
11 pm: What is interesting is how people use internal and external stimuli. Reading, music, other people, looking out the window. Social and solitary.

25 hrs 30 mins

>JEREMY *stands and talks to* FRED.

JEREMY: How are you choosing your route?

>FRED'S *eyes are reflected in the rear view mirror as he makes his reply.*

FRED: I have sort of picked my way right round the edge of it. I've tried to avoid the roundabouts, because those are the things that make you feel a bit woozy. You have probably been round them too many times.

JEREMY: I think, if possible, we should try to keep within the grid. I think Hayley would like the driving to be quite dense.

>*There is a sense of anxiety as* ARCHIE, LUCY *and* JEREMY *discuss the imminent arrival of* MICHAEL.

LUCY: I hear there is a stranger getting on the bus?

ARCHIE: Who is that?

JEREMY: Mike the Gallery Director.

25 hrs 45 mins

AARON *and* PIPPA *are engaged in a prolonged conversation.*

AARON: People that I work with separate the social from the medical model, that is, you are disabled by your parents and by society.

PIPPA: Yes.

AARON: Another writer that I like a lot is Hélène Cixous. I started reading theory when I was thirty.

26 hrs

JEREMY *interjects.*

JEREMY: When do you think we can have another cigarette?

PIPPA: Got another two hours yet.

JEREMY *gets up and walks to the front of the coach.*

JEREMY: Just wondering when your next stop is due?

FRED: We left the restaurant at eight o'clock or thereabouts, then we stopped at Tesco's. It is up to you if you would like to stop.

JEREMY: There are a few restless smokers on board.

FRED: I'll pull into the Marina.

PIPPA: Have you tried patches?

ARCHIE: I tried patches for a while.

PIPPA: It was just more fixation. You only smoke three a day?

ARCHIE: I had a cigarette holder.

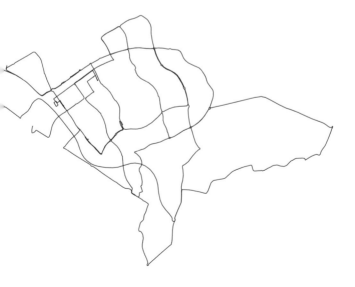

26 hrs 15 mins

33 EXT MILTON KEYNES MARINA.

FRED and PIPPA stand at the water's edge—there are boats in the background—the scene is lit from above by a single streetlamp.

FRED: I am retired really, but I go in teaching a couple of days a week.

JEREMY: What is it you teach?

FRED: Engineering and mainly fabrication – welding at the moment. Only practical things, not a lot to do with theory.

PIPPA: How long have you lived at the Marina?

FRED: Six years.

PIPPA: Fantastic.

FRED: I had a narrow boat but now I have got one of the big plastic boats.

PIPPA: Well, you must love it.

FRED: Yeah, lovely life.

FRED pauses.

FRED: I'll just walk up the end and say hello to the wife.

26 hrs 30 mins

01/04/2006   00:08:04   0.57 kph

PIPPA *strokes a white-haired dog.*

PIPPA: What a beautiful animal.

ARIA, JEREMY, AARON, HAYLEY *and* PIPPA *are seen from a distance—they stand and talk to a man with two white-haired dogs—their speech is inaudible.*

The camera pans slowly along the water's edge—only a couple of boats still have their lights on.

AARON *rolls and lights a cigarette.*

26 hrs 45 mins

01/04/2006   00:23:03   30 kph

34 INT COACH.

Int/ext—view from window.

ARIA: (*Muttering.*) Over and over again and you are not going anywhere and you are not seeing anything interesting. I'm just feeling agitated.

JEREMY and HAYLEY are seated side by side—they both look ahead.

JEREMY: Are you ok?

HAYLEY: Yeah.

Int/ext—road—the markings and streetlights accentuate a vanishing point—a police car passes by with its siren on.

27 hrs

The coach slows down and pulls into a garage forecourt.

FRED *is on the phone.*

FRED: I am outside the Shell garage.

AARON *raises his right hand as if hailing a cab.*

AARON: Taxi for Mr Williamson!

MARK *gets on the coach—he is followed by his son* KYLE.

HAYLEY: Hello Mark.

KYLE *is shy and hovers behind his father.*

MARK: This is my son Kyle.

PIPPA *waves at* KYLE.

PIPPA: Hello Kyle.

HAYLEY: You two *can't* be related!

MARK *puts his bag in the overhead storage and walks to the back of the coach.*

MARK: I am going to make sure that the coffee machine is full, so we don't run out of coffee during the journey.

27 hrs 15 mins

*The coach is on the move again—*PIPPA *is taking a photo of* ARIA.

PIPPA: Go on, smoulder, baby, smoulder …

ARIA *looks at a Polaroid of* AARON.

ARIA: You look like a terrorist.

AARON *looks at* ARIA'S *emerging image.*

AARON: You look a little bit like Freddie Mercury.

ARIA: You should have seen me when I had a moustache, I got told that a lot. Either that or The Village People.

ARCHIE *looks through the camera's viewfinder—he is preparing to take a photo of* PIPPA.

PIPPA *positions herself and gets ready to have her photo taken.*

PIPPA: Can I at least take my glasses off? I usually have my eyes shut. Tell me when you are ready.

ARCHIE *takes a photo of* PIPPA.

27 hrs 30 mins

Os—the sound of a packet being opened—someone is munching on crisps.

AARON *and* ARIA *are looking at a Polaroid photo of* PIPPA.

AARON: You have got the secret of eternal youth.

ARIA: Exactly. Let's get her.

AARON: Wow! You look like an angel, the angel of Milton Keynes.

ARIA: You look about eighteen in that picture.

The camera zooms in on the photo of PIPPA.

PIPPA: Ah, it is great, isn't it? Not that I can see anything because I haven't got my glasses on. To me I look eighteen in *all* the pictures.

AARON: Have you been drinking bat serum?

PIPPA: Bat serum? Every night.

PIPPA *stands—she picks up two empty coffee cups.*

PIPPA: I am just going to take these back here.

PIPPA *walks to the back of the coach.*

27 hrs 45 mins

MEECHY *is at the back of the coach—he suddenly sees* MARK'S *son* KYLE *in the driver's hold—*KYLE *is watching a DVD and eating chocolate.*

MEECHY: (*Shouts.*) There is a stowaway child in there! (*To* KYLE.) What film are you watching?

KYLE: *'Star Wars I'.*

HAYLEY *sits behind* MARK *at the front of the coach.*

MARK: You have covered 540 miles so far.

HAYLEY: Haven't even got to Edinburgh.

MARK: This is going to end on April the first by the way.

ARIA *sips wine.*

ARIA: April Fool!

Int/ext—the road is lit by the coach's headlights.

MARK: My aim is to add as many new roads as possible, so here is your first one.

JEREMY: How about driveways? Oh, this is great.

MARK: What do you want? Big houses or council houses?

28 hrs

MARK *is now driving round a car park.*

JEREMY: That's it, you have got the idea. Until you get a ticket.

MARK: Do you want a squiggly line in it as well? A nice little curvy line?

MARK *drives round and round—he is trying to draw curves with the coach.*

JEREMY: Unfortunately I think these kinds of squiggles might be too small. I appreciate the effort.

MARK: Ok, I will make them bigger.

MARK *begins to draw larger curves with the bus—the camera's LCD screen relays what is seen.*

HAYLEY: It looks great on camera.

Int/ext—car park.

28 hrs 15 mins

01/04/2006   01:53:03   20 kph

MARK: This is where the Poundstretcher advert is done. You know? The one where they drop the pound in the car park?

HAYLEY: I haven't seen it.

MARK: A big pound sign – it's just cut in half or whatever.

> MARK *continues to drive round the car park—the coach headlights fall on a kissing couple.*

HAYLEY: A little bit of snoggage going on there.

MARK: I wonder if we will get done for dogging? Who is in charge of the GPS?

HAYLEY: Jeremy.

MARK: Jeremy, we are blaming you if we get done for dogging.

JEREMY: Group dogging?

MARK: Careful. There are children on board, me included.

> *A person staggers across the car park.*

HAYLEY: *Drunk*!

28 hrs 30 mins

HAYLEY *and* MARK *are seen from behind.*

MARK: Where do you come from originally?

HAYLEY: Turvey.

MARK: Ah, right. Bedford.

HAYLEY: The postcode was a Milton Keynes postcode: MK43!

HAYLEY *and* MARK *are seen from the front.*

MARK: How was the singing guitarist at the gallery on the night you left?

HAYLEY: He had an air tank and was singing underwater.

MARK: When I looked through I could see the big bin there, which I assumed was full of water?

HAYLEY: Yes, there was a big mirror in the lid and you could see him while he was performing underwater.

01/04/2006   02:23:00   13 kph

MARK: You'd think driving around like this, it would be quite easy to become disorientated.

Int/ext—road—a fairground comes into shot—there is a big wheel—voices continue os.

MARK: Ohhh, look at that!

HAYLEY: It is moving.

MARK: Yeah, shall we stop?

HAYLEY: Hey! Look at the fair. We are going to the fair! Brilliant driver, genius driver.

MARK: It is just slowing down. You could probably get it on the camera.

AARON: Bloody hell. Can we have a go on that?

MARK slows down—he positions the coach so that the fixed camera at the front of the coach can video the fairground ride.

HAYLEY: The bus film-maker.

MARK: Sorry officer, but I am doing this in the name of art.

The coach starts moving again.

ARIA: The driver's not drunk, but I am.

A member of the public sees the coach being driven round the car park—he stands and scratches his head in astonishment.

JEREMY: Look at that poor confused person.

HAYLEY: The people are just like, 'What the fuck?'

29 hrs

01/04/2006   02:38:00   20 kph

A large man runs across the road.

HAYLEY: Get drunk and get your beer goggles on.

Int/ext—window—the camera tracks past a pyramid-shaped glass building.

HAYLEY: The Point cinema looks so sad. It doesn't look like a point any more. It's pointless!

MARK: They call it 'The Red Leany' now.

AARON *reaches for his guitar.*

ARIA: Oh no, Aaron has got his guitar out.

HAYLEY: He won't play during the day! It's my fault, I bought him that guitar for his fortieth birthday.

AARON *starts twanging his guitar.*

HAYLEY: I remember the shopping centre and the car park before The Point was built.

MARK: Well I just remember The Point because you used to be able to see it from the road.

29 hrs 15 mins

01/04/2006   02:53:01   30 kph

A drunken man is leaning against a wall—he holds up a red rose in an attempt to 'hail' the coach.

MARK: Look at the state of that.

HAYLEY: That's a great suit. What do you mean?

ARIA: Maybe we should follow someone else's car, keep following people until they get really pissed off.

The drunken man is caught in the coach headlights—he walks toward the coach in the style of Charlie Chaplin.

JEREMY: Hello, hello.

The coach turns right and is driven around the man.

JEREMY: That was great. How much is it to get a bus licence?

29 hrs 30 mins

01/04/2006   03:08:28   85 kph

    MARK *drives the coach into another car park.*

AARON: Jesus wept, we'll be driving through allotments soon.

    The drunk staggers in the distance—he is following the coach.

MARK: Do you think he is a little bit tipsy?

JEREMY: He is thinking, 'What the fuck is a coach doing down here?'

    The drunk walks away from the coach into the distance.

MARK: Oh, he got quite a way.

MARK: There is a police car. Let's disappear and go in here.

    The coach turns right out of the car park and onto the road.

29 hrs 45 mins

HAYLEY, MARK *and* JEREMY *continue talking—they look exhausted and are desperately trying to stay awake by making small talk.*

MARK: You know there is a Springfield here?

HAYLEY: Does Homer Simpson live here also?

MARK: No, but there is a Simpson as well.

JEREMY: I think there is a Springfield in almost every state in America.

MARK: Milton Keynes also has easyPizza as well as easyCinema.

HAYLEY *and* JEREMY *act repulsed.*

HAYLEY/JEREMY: (*Together.*) Urghghgh.

MARK: What is wrong with that?

30 hrs

35 EXT PETROL STATION FORECOURT.

PIPPA *gets off the coach and joins* ARIA, LUCY, HAYLEY *and* AARON *on the station forecourt—they walk around stretching their legs.*

*The forecourt is brightly-lit and empty—*JEREMY *goes to the shop to buy something—the* PARTICIPANTS *get back on the coach.*

30 hrs 15 mins

36 INT COACH.

*The coach is stationary—*KYLE *is speaking to his father* MARK.

KYLE: Dad, can I have one of your mini-eggs?

MARK *makes coffee with his back to the camera.*

MARK: No, you have got your own food.

KYLE: Can I honk the horn, Dad?

MARK: No you can't. After 11pm it is illegal.

MARK *walks down the aisle to the front of the coach and sits down at the wheel.*

JEREMY: Can you not drive so fast this time? Just slow it down. We are getting a bit sick in the back there.

MARK *sits with his hands on the wheel.*

MARK: Have we got everyone? Everyone on board?

The engine is started and the trip is underway again.

30 hrs 30 mins

HAYLEY: One of the first designs for Milton Keynes was called Pooleville, thought up by someone called Poole. The new city was to be built round a monorail in the shape of a figure-of-eight, an eternity symbol.

JEREMY: That would have been a disaster. Disastrous.

HAYLEY: That was rejected and they then built the city round the LA grid format. I'm in the Pooleville camp myself.

Streetlights flash by.

JEREMY: It would quickly outgrow itself. There would only be a certain amount of capacity that could be put on that monorail.

MARK: I am surprised that for the new city, when they first did it, they didn't incorporate a tram system.

HAYLEY: Perhaps they didn't foresee an oil crisis? It is now estimated that oil peak will occur in 2010.

MARK: They don't have trams in LA do they?

JEREMY: They used to have trains, but they sold the rail networks to the car companies who paved them over.

01/04/2006   04:23:01   23 kph

    MARK *starts telling a new story.*

MARK: There is a good little story here. They wanted to build a big recycling plant up the back of Bletchley. The local council denied planning permission, the locals opposed it and everything else. They said that the road infrastructure wasn't good enough to have all the lorries trouncing up and down.

    *Int/ext—road—*MARK'S *voice continues os.*

MARK: All of a sudden this stretch of road appeared and it goes nowhere. They haven't got their site yet, but of course I reckon when they reapply in five years' time there will be no argument. But you can see this is it now. We have come to the end.

    The coach turns off the road.

JEREMY: It is like a drag strip.

01/04/2006   04:38:01   23 kph

31 hrs 15 mins

01/04/2006   04:53:04   25 kph

The PARTICIPANTS *are quiet*—MARK *is listening to the radio*—
the interior lights have been switched off—*most of the*
PARTICIPANTS *are asleep or dozing*—EDNA *is lying across the*
back seat—JEREMY *walks to the back of the coach*—PIPPA
looks bored—ARIA *rests his head on a pile of crossword puzzles*
and MEECHY *sits upright with his eyes closed.*

31 hrs 30 mins

RADIO: If you like the music of The Soggy Bottom Boys,
I have got more Soggy Bottoms for you over the next hour.
You are going to like that. *You* are choosing the songs and
this is 'Man of Constant Sorrow'.

MARK'S *hands are seen turning the steering wheel.*

The coach stops—MARK *switches the engine off and secures
the handbrake.*

JEREMY: Are you alright?

MARK: Yeah. Just need a bit of shut-eye.

MARK *turns down the radio and shuts his eyes—he falls asleep
immediately.*

*Int/ext—road—the coach is parked in a petrol station
forecourt—the forecourt is recognisable, the coach has been
here before.*

31 hrs 45 mins

01/04/2006   05:23:03   0.67 kph

Birds are heard singing os.

A lorry passes in front of the coach.

The sky gets brighter—it is raining lightly—there are no cars on the road.

32 hrs

MARK *has woken up. He wipes his eyes, yawns and stretches before switching the radio on again.*

RADIO: Milton Keynes can't cope with the amount it is expanding. Green Party campaigner Helen Francis has told Horizon Radio that our city is being developed too much and it is bad news for our villages.

MARK *starts the coach and drives off the station forecourt.*

RADIO: There is only one Milton Keynes. Horizon Radio 103.3 FM. This is Bob Dylan with 'One More Cup of Coffee'. It is twenty minutes to six.

32 hrs 15 mins

01/04/2006   05:53:59   24 kph

Lucy's Diary
6 am: When I woke up I was the only one awake, apart from the
bus driver, which I quite enjoyed. I thought how ironic it would
be if the coach stopped now and I was the only witness.

32 hrs 30 mins

    MARK *is speaking on the phone.*

MARK: Morning.

    MARK *listens to another person at the end of the line.*

MARK: Just about. (*Pause.*) Shattered. (*Pause.*) Just coming up to 1,000 kilometres/630 miles. If Tony's estimation is right, and it does twelve hours on a tank, that's 1,200 kilometres. So, there is another 200 kilometres to go. Plus, he doesn't want to leave it totally empty. Have you left yet? Yeah? What are you going to do? Alright. Oh right. Wonderful. Thanks. Ok.

    The diesel gauge shows that the tank is three-quarters empty.

32 hrs 45 mins

01/04/2006   06:23:03   67 kph

*Int/ext—window—the verge is reflected in the wing mirror—
the light is cool.*

RADIO: We are a new club in a new area. We want the whole
community to be involved. That would reflect the diversity of
Milton Keynes and we feel it is important that this is reflected
in the spectators attending the game. It was confirmed yesterday
that Wembley won't be ready in time to host the gigs, but it
is going to save us a lot of time and money. Not everyone is
disappointed that Take That and Bon Jovi have had to switch
their gigs to the Milton Keynes Bowl. Student Debbie says
she doesn't care where the gig is as long as she gets to watch
Take That.

33 hrs

Lucy's Diary
6:45 am: We're beginning to anticipate the end of the journey
and have all guessed a time for when the bus will stop. Until now
I hadn't taken any notice of how much petrol was left but it's
becoming something we pay attention to. It's like a child asking,
'Are we there yet?'

33 hrs 15 mins

37 EXT COACH—EARLY MORNING.

The camera trucks along the verge and houses can be seen through the trees.

High angle: from bridge—the coach is driven under the bridge.

Low angle: the blue of the sky is reflected in the road—vehicles pass left to right.

A few pedestrians are seen walking on the pavement.

The camera trucks along a long stretch of road.

33 hrs 30 mins

01/04/2006   07:08:10   62 kph

38 INT COACH.

MARK: (*On phone.*) There is a car overturned near the hospital, but you won't be going near there will you? Yeah, I've done all the 'H's and I'm on the V's at the moment. Cheers. Later.

Heavy rain.

PIPPA *looks bleary.*

PIPPA: Have we stopped recently?

MARK: We stopped about an hour ago.

PIPPA *looks out of the window.*

RADIO: A thief has stolen a car with a baby in it. The mother was recycling glass at the time. Police officers, dog handlers and helicopters joined the search.

33 hrs 45 mins

01/04/2006   07:23:58   24 kph

MARK: (*On phone.*) Have you got any motion sickness tablets?

The diesel gauge is still at three-quarters empty.

RADIO: Stowe House Wedding Exhibition. There is one place you should be heading this weekend. There will be hair and make-up exhibitions to make sure you look beautiful for your special day.

The speedometer reads 45 kph.

RADIO: Motor Serve – everything for the motorist.

The water gauge light is flashing on the dashboard.

RADIO: It's big, real big, the big deal sale at the Co-op, your department store.

MARK *indicates left.*

MARK: (*On phone.*) Shell garage? Err, well I am at Wolverton Station, V6 or 5. They are all starting to wake up now. Ok, right, you might be there before me. See you soon.

RADIO: At breakfast next week, you can earn Nectar points from Sainsbury's. Thousands of rewards are sweeter with Nectar on Horizon Radio, 103.3 FM.

MARK'S *hands are on the steering wheel—we see his foot press down on the accelerator.*

34 hrs

>   HAYLEY *has just woken up—she stands behind* MARK.

HAYLEY: Buon Giorno Monsieur! That was a very nice sleep, much needed. So, what's the state of play?

MARK: Well, you missed an overturned car, police and fire engines. Should all be on the video. Is it Jeremy that is doing the GPS? He noticed that the video wasn't recording during the night. He has re-started it. The whole thing had switched off.

HAYLEY: Hmm, it has done that before. As soon as you take your eye off it, it switches itself off.

MARK: It was recording for the accident anyway.

>   JEREMY *walks to the front of the coach—*MEECHY *reads—*
>   ARIA *makes coffee—*EDNA *files her nails—*HAYLEY *puts out*
>   *her hand to stabilise herself as the coach swings round a*
>   *corner—*ARCHIE *dozes—*ARIA *hands* MARK *a cup of coffee.*

34 hrs 15 mins

01/04/2006   07:53:40   67 kph

LUCY: I think everyone should be woken up.

PIPPA: They shouldn't be sleeping now, not on the last day.

HAYLEY *interjects.*

HAYLEY: What does the petrol look like Mark?

MARK: Usually a yellowy-orange colour.

The coach judders.

HAYLEY: Sorry, what does the diesel gauge look like Mark?

MARK: Erm, black with a white wibbly thing in it.

KYLE: How much petrol is left?

MARK: None.

HAYLEY: Ask him how much diesel is left.

MARK: A little bit.

Int/ext—road.

34 hrs 30 mins

01/04/2006   08:08:46   42 kph

A live feed of the road is seen on the LCD screen.

*The radio plays 'Crawling from the Wreckage' by
Graham Parker.*

RADIO: 'Got out early from the factory, driving like a nut, but
I didn't see that thing until it came'.

*The camera focuses on the butterfly print on the back of one
of the seats—it pans down before zooming in on a pile of sweet
wrappers—*JEREMY *reaches to switch on the air conditioning.*

RADIO: 'Crawling from the wreckage, you'd think that by now
at least, a half my brain would get the message'.

MEECHY *is listening to music on his headphones—*AARON
*gets up and moves around the coach—*HAYLEY *leans her head
against the window and looks down.*

RADIO: 'Crawling from the wreckage and into a brand new car'.

PIPPA *puts her hand on* KYLE'S *head and whispers into his ear.*

34 hrs 45 mins

01/04/2006   08:23:14   67 kph

    KYLE *pulls on* PIPPA'S *sleeve.*

KYLE: How many photos have you got of me now?

PIPPA: I've only got a couple of you.

    Int/ext—road—it is light.

HAYLEY: Mark, what time are we going to stop for breakfast?

MARK: About nine. I don't know where you want to go?

HAYLEY: IKEA!

ARIA: (*Shouts.*) I think they should give us free stuff.

MARK: Oh, fine.

35 hrs

KYLE *is sitting with all his stuff around him: DVDs, comics, sweets.*

HAYLEY: (*To* KYLE.) Well that might be the case. Doesn't mean you are not gorgeous and beautiful. (*To* MARK.) Kyle asked if he can call his mum.

MARK: He knows that at half-past eight she will kill him! She is not awake then.

KYLE *grizzles.*

KYLE: What time can I call her?

MARK: After 10 am.

35 hrs 15 mins

> HAYLEY *and* PIPPA *sway from side to side singing 'Those Were the Days, My Friend'.*

> KYLE *doesn't like their singing—he scrunches up his face and puts his fingers in his ears.*

KYLE: Bad singers.

PIPPA: How could you be so rude!

KYLE: I want my money back.

PIPPA: We are usually paid *not* to sing.

> HAYLEY *gets up to answer her mobile phone—as she does so she moves away from* PIPPA *and* KYLE.

HAYLEY: Mike, hiya. We are still driving around. Yup, we are going to head for IKEA for a 9 am break if we don't run out of petrol … err diesel – sorry Mark! – first.

> HAYLEY *turns to* MARK.

HAYLEY: Mark, do you think we will make it to IKEA?

35 hrs 30 mins

01/04/2006   09:08:21   26 kph

    ARIA *points out of the window.*

ARIA: I know that guy, his name is James, he works at …

    HAYLEY *talks to* JUSTIN *on her mobile.*

HAYLEY: Justin, hi. We are meeting Mike at IKEA for breakfast at nine. Would you like to join us there?

    *The bus judders—*ARIA *and* PIPPA *continue talking.*

ARIA: I think we have about four churches here. This area has the worst reputation, you know, for being rough. Our local venue is just behind here: it is a school. I've been going there since I was fourteen. They used to have a curfew, so what we would do was turn up, buy a ticket to the gig, but end up getting trashed.

KYLE: Is that a school?

HAYLEY: The back end of one.

    LUCY *laughs out loud.*

LUCY: I haven't seen this roundabout before!

    Int/ext—road—the coach speeds up—it starts to rain again.

35 hrs 45 mins

ARIA: There is a guy that makes one hundred percent synthetic perfumes. Some of them are copies of perfumes that already exist, others are natural smells like rhubarb. I really like the rhubarb one.

    HAYLEY *and* PIPPA *face forward.*

KYLE: I am going to put my shoes on.

PIPPA: Have you made your pit?

    KYLE *stands.*

PIPPA: I wonder if we should buy the newspaper report that came out on Thursday?

ARIA: I saw one that was being used.

HAYLEY: I think they will write about the coach trip next week.

ARIA: I don't think they will. It's not current news.

36 hrs

39 EXT IKEA CAR PARK.

MICHAEL *and his* FAMILY *get out of their car.*

JUSTIN *drives into shot—he stops his car and gets out.*

The PARTICIPANTS *get off the coach—they rub their eyes as they enter the sunshine.*

40 INT IKEA CANTEEN.

EDNA, LUCY *and* ARCHIE *stand at the counter—*KYLE *and* PIPPA *queue behind.*

ARCHIE: (*Addressing* LUCY.) After you.

EDNA *walks toward* PIPPA—KYLE *bends down to pick something up.*

JEREMY *and* ARIA *are in the eating area arranging chairs and tables.*

EDNA *puts her tray down on the table—*HAYLEY *and* LUCY *join her.*

36 hrs 15 mins

MICHAEL *opens a yogurt pot and hands it to his daughter—* MEECHY *reaches for the salt and pepper—* JUSTIN *is recording the breakfast on his video camera.*

JUSTIN *pov shot:* HAYLEY *and* AARON *are talking—* HAYLEY *lip speaks and does not use her voice—* LUCY *and* HAYLEY *laugh.*

PIPPA *and* KYLE *are seated opposite each other.*

KYLE: I've been drinking hot chocolate.

The camera dollies left along the table—it turns and dollies back in the opposite direction.

ARIA *leans forward and sniffs his breakfast.*

ARIA: A very Swedish smell.

36 hrs 30 mins

41 INT IKEA TOILETS.

HAYLEY *and* PIPPA *stand in front of a toilet mirror.*

*They both wash their hands—*HAYLEY *looks in the mirror—
her eyes fill with tears—*HAYLEY *wipes the tears away from
her eyes—*PIPPA *offers* HAYLEY *some support.*

HAYLEY: Sorry. I'm just feeling a bit emotional.

The camera slowly dollies behind HAYLEY *and* PIPPA *as they
leave the toilets.*

01/04/2006   10:23:38   50 kph

42 INT COACH.

MICHAEL & KIDS *have joined the group on the coach.*

JEREMY *is looking around—he has lost something.*

MICHAEL *points at the pile of DVDs on the table.*

MICHAEL: Did you watch any of the movies?

LUCY *laughs.*

HAYLEY: What has he got? A straw …?

Indistinct chatter.

LUCY *and* HAYLEY *stand.*

37 hrs

PIPPA *sits reading the newspaper*—EDNA *joins her.*

MICHAEL *gets out felt-tip pens and paper and gives them to his children.*

HAYLEY *holds up a piece of A4 paper.*

HAYLEY: Oh yeah, see if you can get everyone's email on it. I've already got Lucy, Aria and Jeremy.

JEREMY *laughs as he looks at the sheet of paper on the table.*

JEREMY: What font is that?

HAYLEY: That is called 'coach' font! They should invent a typeface called 'Coach' that is all wobbly and looks like it has been written on a bus.

MARK *is excited.*

MARK: I have seen a few cars pointing at us, saying, 'Oh, there it is'.

KYLE: When are you next going on the wavy road?

MARK: I am not.

KYLE: Why?

MARK: Because I am concentrating on running out of diesel.

AARON *plays 'Born to be Wild' in 3/4 time on his guitar.*

MARK *reaches forward and turns up the radio and drowns* AARON *out.*

RADIO: Stave off the cold with some great music on the radio and whatever you are doing around Milton Keynes, drop me a line about it and we will get some Saturday 'shout outs' for you.

JEREMY *raises an eyebrow.*

JEREMY: There we go. Anyone doing anything in MK today?

MARK: Yes.

AARON *gives* KYLE *his guitar—*KYLE *tries to play the guitar and the children sing 'The wheels on the bus go round and round'.*

The coach stalls.

37 hrs 15 mins

01/04/2006   10:53:18   61 kph

Int/ext—road—it is sunny.

Indistinct chatter can be heard in the background.

RADIO: It is just coming up to twenty to eleven. There is a bizarre thing going on today. A coach is travelling round Milton Keynes for as long as it can. We have got Mark on the phone from New City Coaches. He has been driving round in the coach for thirty-seven hours. How's it going Mark?

MARK: It is going very well, thank you.

RADIO: Where have you been?

MARK: Round the whole grid system, all the villages, everywhere really, fifty, sixty, seventy times over by the feel of it.

RADIO: So where are you now?

MARK: Just coming up to the city centre, heading down to the bus depot at the moment.

RADIO: Okey dokey, and who have you got on the bus with you? Are there a lot of people on the coach?

MARK: Yes, yes. They are all 'artistes' of one sort or another.

RADIO: And what will happen when you run out of petrol?

LUCY: (*To the* PARTICIPANTS.) We get off!

MARK: Hopefully, erm, I'll be glad to get rid of them by then! No, that is part of the project. Basically, where it stops is where it finishes and that is where they finish.

RADIO: Okey dokey. If you are driving round MK, what do you look like?

MARK: It is a long white coach with 'New City Coaches' written all over it.

RADIO: Seems like you have got another hour to go. I hope it goes well for you.

MARK: Cheers Emma. Bye-bye.

RADIO: Bye. Oh my goodness, what a way to spend a Saturday morning.

MARK: (*Points at a Milton Keynes yellow bus.*) That lot on the bus just pointed at us.

RADIO: Thank you to Mark and all you guys on the coach. Thirty-seven hours on a coach. I can't think of anything worse. I hope there is a toilet on there.

37 hrs 30 mins

01/04/2006   11:08:14   0.29 kph

The coach stops.

MICHAEL *and* KIDS, *and* KYLE *and* MARK *prepare to get off the coach.*

MICHAEL: Bye bye. Take care.

JEREMY *looks at his GPS unit.*

JEREMY: Actually, the April Fools' joke is that it won't run out.

HAYLEY'S *mobile phone rings—it is* JUSTIN.

HAYLEY: Justin just told me that the coach is blowing out black smoke.

MARK *is saying goodbye to* IAN.

IAN: I'll be glad when this weekend is over.

MARK: Think of the money.

JEREMY *shakes* MARK'S *hand.*

JEREMY: Thanks for all your roundabouteering.

Int/ext—road—it is sunny.

IAN: Let's get moving and run it out of diesel. Do you want to stay close to the city, Hayley?

HAYLEY: Yeah.

37 hrs 45 mins

01/04/2006   11:23:08   0.09 kph

All the PARTICIPANTS *are seated at the front of the coach.*

HAYLEY: Mike and I went to Ladbrokes and tried to place a bet on when the coach would stop. They said that if we had told them five days ago they could have arranged it. We were just too late, so let's do it here instead!

HAYLEY *changes her focus and points to the list in front of her.*

HAYLEY: So, Edna, you came in at 10:40. Can you imagine the gallery feedback form for this? 'It would have been better if we hadn't broken down at the end'.

PIPPA: My daughter is a policewoman. She is going to come and try to find me.

HAYLEY: Can she arrest me for bad art?

PIPPA *speaks to her daughter on a mobile.*

PIPPA: Ahhh, do you only wear your uniform when you are on duty? Couldn't you pretend you had just finished work? What, you have to leave your uniform in your locker? But we are driving around and can't stop. You will just have to drive past us and wave! Ok, darling. Bye!

38 hrs

01/04/2006   11:38:06   38 kph

JEREMY *looks at his watch.*

JEREMY: 11:45.

LUCY: Only a quarter to twelve?

The group is quiet.

JEREMY: It is like the beginning.

LUCY: What is your name again?

JEREMY: Hi, I'm the GPS guy!

LUCY: No you are not, your name is Jeremy!

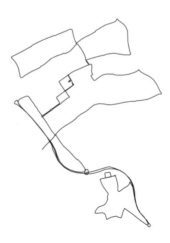

38 hrs 15 mins

01/04/2006   11:53:00   37 kph

    AARON *starts singing.*

AARON: 'Three wheels on my wagon and I'm still rolling along'.

JEREMY: 'Six wheels on my wagon ...'

    PIPPA *looks through her photos.*

PIPPA: Edna and the dummy.

    PIPPA *turns to* EDNA—LUCY *crosses her fingers, arms and legs.*

LUCY: Breakdown now – on a roundabout.

    A passing car beeps its horn.

RADIO: And here is the song you have all been waiting for: 'The End' by The Doors.

HAYLEY: I'm just looking for ... (HAYLEY *looks in her bag.*) I have some cab numbers in here somewhere.

RADIO: 'The blue bus is callin' us, driver where you takin' us?'

| END TIME | MILEAGE |

	END TIME	MILEAGE
Jeremy	3pm	
Pippa	3.27 pm	
~~Lucy~~	12.45	760m.
~~Edna~~	~~10.40 am~~	
Arin	4pm	
~~Ashley~~ Archie	12.15pm	
Meechy	9pm	
Justin		
Aaron	310pm	
~~Hayley~~	11.15 am	x
KYLE	12:30 PM	

31/03/06

7.55pm

12.22

Just off A5

38 hrs 30 mins

01/04/2006   12:08:00   72 kph

The diesel gauge is at zero.

RADIO: 'This is the end, beautiful friend'.

IAN: I think that is your lot.

RADIO: 'This is the end'.

ALL: Really!

RADIO: 'My only friend, the end'.

IAN: No, not really.

HAYLEY looks at her watch.

HAYLEY: April Fool. No, you've passed it. It is past midday.

LUCY points to the back of the bus.

LUCY: What happened to Tim?

AARON: I got fed up of being freaked out by it every time I went up the back. I knew it would be a doddle. Creepy, isn't it?

HAYLEY: The question is, how do we tie his head back on?

The coach passes a service station.

JEREMY: Can we have more fuel?

The sound of one long beep followed by three short beeps is heard as the engine cuts out and the coach stops.

IAN: You just ran out of fuel.

Everyone cheers.

JEREMY: Really, that's it?

LUCY: What time is it? Who won?

ALL: Kyle won.

LUCY: Very tasteful, wasn't it?

ARIA: I thought it would be more juddery.

HAYLEY: What is the time exactly?

LUCY: 12:22 by my watch.

JEREMY: Can I get off?

HAYLEY: You don't need my permission to get off.

43 EXT ROADSIDE—MILTON KEYNES BOWL.

ARCHIE: We are at Shenley Lodge/Cockrill Hill, just off the A5.

HAYLEY: Ian, do we need to ring the police?

IAN: No. Should be alright.

AARON: Is someone going to come and fetch us?

PIPPA: Where did they say we were?

HAYLEY: I think Shenley Lodge.

PIPPA: (*Speaking on mobile.*) Right, we have just broken down. I think Shenley Lodge, and I think it is the other side of town.

ARIA: I won't tell anyone.

PIPPA: (*Speaking on mobile.*) Well we are here, wherever we are. We don't know where we are. Hang on, I'll just find out.

ARIA: We are near Shenley Lodge.

EDNA: Just by Watling Street, V4.

PIPPA: (*Speaking on mobile.*) Watling Street, V4? We don't know quite yet how we are getting home. Taxis or what? Is it the wrong side to you? Ok. Bye.

MEECHY: Shall we get a photo of us all pushing the bus?

PIPPA: What do you think everyone is doing?

HAYLEY: Let's just wait a minute because Ian is just sorting the coach out.

ARIA: Have we hired the driver per day or per hour?

EDNA: The gallery will pay for our taxis back. I need to get one. Do we have a number for a taxi?

PIPPA: Taxi – ask Hayley.

EDNA: Excuse me, you don't have a taxi number?

IAN: Sixty-nine, sixty-nine, sixty-nine.

HAYLEY: I have all the taxi codes. I need the exact address. Do you know where we are exactly?

IAN: At the side of the MK Bowl.

HAYLEY: OK, I'll call. Meechy, where do you need to go?

MEECHY: Newport Pagnell.

AARON: That's the Milton Keynes Bowl.

JEREMY: What's inside?

AARON: The Rolling Stones played there.

JEREMY: They play anywhere.

    IAN *tries the engine. It starts.*

LUCY: It's working!

    IAN *revs the engine.*

HAYLEY: You are done, are you?

ARCHIE: We expected it would take an hour or something.

JEREMY: *(Shouting.)* Can you give us a ride back to the gallery?

IAN: Yes, I expect so.

MEECHY: (*To* HAYLEY.) A picture of you in front of the bus?

IAN: Back to the gallery.

MEECHY: Like a prisoner being released, I can't stand the open world.

IAN: I'll just ring and tell Mark the good news. (*To* MARK.) Hello. I have run out and restarted …

Lucy's Diary

12:20 pm: Finally the bus glided to a halt by the side of a dual carriageway just before a roundabout. It was exciting, though not spectacular, and an anticlimax at the same time. Jumped off and ran around with glee.

THE END

PIPPA: I felt really disappointed when we got back on the bus and drove back to the gallery. That was the one thing that I was left with when I came away. I just wanted it to … to die! And then we would have to find another way of getting back.

HAYLEY: I was thinking, I wonder if they expect me to do anything to mark the point at which the bus breaks down, because I haven't got anything planned.

PIPPA: Yeah.

HAYLEY: The idea had always been for the bus to breakdown and for us to find our own way home, but everything happened so quickly at that point. Actually, I don't know if it happened quickly?

PIPPA: It felt like everything was happening very quickly. I don't think that it was as quick as we may remember it.

HAYLEY: The driver pumped the engine, put some diesel in and got the bus up and running in a few minutes. The original idea was that people would walk home. But Edna was very tired and had to get home. At that point the bus driver offered to give us a lift back to the gallery. It felt almost unnatural to say no.

PIPPA: Why?

HAYLEY: Because we had become institutionalised by the bus! Everything about the ending was anticlimactic. The coach didn't splutter. It just cut out.

PIPPA: It kind of just expired.

HAYLEY: It is interesting that you felt depressed by the ending. I agree, it was very strange.

PIPPA: There was a kind of chaos to it that I really liked.

HAYLEY: Are you talking about something to do with the fact that the driver took over and was in control at the end? I don't want to get metaphysical, but there was something death-like about the end point. And there was definitely something professional and in control about the manner of the bus driver. He was like a doctor. He started doing things quite mechanistically: pumping the engine, filling it up, ticking over the engine again. He had a system in place.

PIPPA: I found what you were wearing with your scarf really striking. I felt like you ought to have a little bag!

HAYLEY: I was unconsciously dressed like an air hostess. Perhaps that was part of my persona, facilitating the journey for everyone?

PIPPA: I think what happened in there was incredibly important because of the relationships. Relationships are hugely important towards sustainability. I think that it's all very well thinking about all the other issues that encompass it, but actually relationships between people I think are the most important things we should be working on. Erm, that sounds really …

HAYLEY: No, it doesn't!

PIPPA: That's what I have felt because those relationships can be worked upon and changed, and this piece actually welcomes that difference.

HAYLEY: Yeah. I've got some questions to ask about when we sat around the table as we were waiting for the bus to stop. What do you think about that? I found it kind of comforting to be together. It wasn't sad.

PIPPA: No, not as a group. I'm not sure that sitting together was comforting but I think that's when I pulled back a bit because it was coming to an end. Like you, I felt very emotional in the IKEA toilets! I mean, who wouldn't!

HAYLEY: The point at which I cried in the IKEA toilets was the most emotional, then I cut myself off.

PIPPA: I find it really intriguing that you can make connections with some people and it is almost as if you have known them inside for such a long time, that you have really connected, and you can do that within half an hour. But with other people it takes longer and then with a group you have got all the other different dynamics.

HAYLEY: As the person that facilitated this trip, I was aware of the connections that people were making, but had to stand slightly outside those relationships. It wasn't until the end of the trip that I could relax and get to know people.

Published on the occasion of
Hayley Newman: MKVH (Milton Keynes Vertical Horizontal)
28 March – 1 April 2006

MKVH was originally commissioned by Rules and Regs in partnership
with Milton Keynes Gallery. This publication is generously supported by
Chelsea College of Art and Design, University of the Arts, London.

Milton Keynes Gallery
900 Midsummer Boulevard
Central Milton Keynes MK9 3QA
Telephone: +44 (0)1908 676 900
Fax: +44 (0)1908 558 308
Email: info@mk-g.org
Website: www.mk-g.org
Registered Charity No. 1059678

Distributed by Cornerhouse Publications
70 Oxford Street, Manchester M1 5NH
Telephone: +44 (0)161 200 1503
Fax: +44 (0)161 200 1504
Email: publications@cornerhouse.org
Website: www.cornerhouse.org/publications

ISBN: 978-0-9557610-0-3

Editors: Emma Dean, Cathy Haynes and Michael Stanley
Assistant Editor: Giselle Richardson
Design: Fraser Muggeridge studio
Print: Die Keure

Image Credits/Photography
Aria Alagha, Archie Alexander-Sinclair, Emma Dean, Fred Dedman,
Meechy, Fraser Muggeridge, Hayley Newman, Lucy Turner,
Aaron Williamson and Jeremy Wood.

Hayley Newman and Milton Keynes Gallery would like to extend
special thanks to: Aria Alagha, Archie Alexander-Sinclair, Clive Caswell,
Tamsin Dillon, Tony Grisoni, Janet Hodgson, Robin Klassnik, Seth Kriebel,
Kaffe Matthews, Meechy (www.meechy.net), Justin Neal, Jacqui Newman,
Pippa North, Edna Read, Tim and effigy, Lucy Turner, Aaron Williamson
and Jeremy Wood (www.gpsdrawing.com), Mark Cutler, Kyle Cutler,
Fred Dedman, Ian Marshall and Tony White from New City Coaches.

Milton Keynes Gallery gratefully acknowledges annual revenue support
from Arts Council England, South East, Milton Keynes Council,
English Partnerships and Milton Keynes Theatre & Gallery Company.

Milton Keynes Gallery

Rules and Regs